CHASING PAPER

CHASING PAPER

Critical Reflections
on Christian Books
and Publishing

Edited by
STEPHANIE L. DERRICK

Forewords by
MARK NOLL *and* PHILIP YANCEY

CASCADE *Books* · Eugene, Oregon

CHASING PAPER
Critical Reflections on Christian Books and Publishing

Cascade Books
An Imprint of Wipf and Stock Publishers
199 W. 8th Ave., Suite 3
Eugene, OR 97401

www.wipfandstock.com

PAPERBACK ISBN: 978-1-5326-7758-8
HARDCOVER ISBN: 978-1-5326-7759-5
EBOOK ISBN: 978-1-5326-7760-1

Cataloguing-in-Publication data:

Names: Derrick, Stephanie L., editor. | Noll, Mark, foreword. Yancey, Philip, foreword.

Title: Chasing paper : critical reflections on Christian books and publishing / Edited by Stephanie L. Derrick, forewords by Mark Noll and Philip Yancey.

Description: Eugene, OR: Cascade Books, 2021 | Includes bibliographical references.

Identifiers: ISBN 978-1-5326-7758-8 (paperback) | ISBN 978-1-5326-7759-5 (hardcover) | ISBN 978-1-5326-7760-1 (ebook)

Subjects: LCSH: Christian literature—Publishing. | Church and mass media. | Christian-owned business enterprises. | Publishers and publishing—History—20th century. | Religious literature—Publishing.

Classification: BR115.E3 .C45 2021 (paperback) | BR115.E3 (ebook)

09/27/21

Contents

List of Contributors

Robin Baird-Smith—Publishing Director, Continuum Publishing Group (United Kingdom)

Richard Brown, PhD—Director of the University of South Carolina Press (United States)

Peter Calvin—General Manager of Christian Publishing House (MIK) (Pakistan)

Roy M. Carlisle—Director of Publishing at PageMill (United States)

Mark Carpenter—CEO of Editora Mundo Cristao (Brazil)

Father Giuseppe Costa—Head of The Libreria Editrice Vaticana, 2007–2017 (Italy)

Ian Darke—Coordinator of the Letra Viva network of Latin American Christian publishers (Costa Rica)

Stephanie L. Derrick, PhD—Historian (United States)

Peter Dwyer—Director of Liturgical Press (United States)

Norman A. Hjelm, Teol. Dr.—Senior Theological Editor and Director of Fortress Press, 1974–1978 and 1980–1984 (United States)

Robert Hudson—Senior Editor at Zondervan/HarperCollins, 1984–2018 (United States)

Pieter Kwant—Program Director of Langham Literature (United Kingdom)

Andrew T. Le Peau—Editorial Director, InterVarsity Press, 1985–2016 (United States)

Wonsuk Ma, PhD—Dean and Distinguished Professor of Global Christianity at Oral Roberts University (The Philippines, United Kingdom)

Mark A. Noll, PhD—Professor Emeritus of History at the University of Notre Dame (United States)

Jon Pott—Vice President and Editor-in-Chief, Wm. B. Eerdmans Publishing, 1982–2015 (United States)

Joseph Sinasac—Publishing Director at Novalis Publishing (Canada)

Jon Stock—Publisher at Wipf and Stock Publishers (United States)

Greg Thornton, DDiv (hon) —Senior Vice President of Media at Moody Institute (United States)

Sandra Vander Zicht—Associate Publisher and Executive Editor at Zondervan, 1986–2018 (United States)

C. Jeffrey Wright—Chief Executive Officer, Urban Ministries, Inc. (United States)

Philip Yancey—Author (United States)

MARK NOLL

Foreword

BOOK LOVERS SHOULD LOVE this book. Book lovers who are also authors should *really* love this book.

The memories collected here from editors with long experience in Christian publishing offer much that could be expected, but also quite a bit that might not be anticipated. Men and women who have spent their adult lives trying to make other people's prose as effective as possible turn out, not surprisingly, to write well themselves. Whether describing changing market conditions (the rise of "technological giants"), perspectives on the future ("Farewell to the Golden Age"), shifts in marketing strategy (from the responsibility of the firm to the responsibility of the author), the oft-predicted domination of the ebook (it isn't going to happen), and much more, the editors produce the kind of accessible prose they have so often demanded of their authors. While requesting "clear and succinct" from so many others, they have obviously taken their own words to heart.

As might also be expected, their range of editing experiences illuminates a wide range of publishing pathways. As an author who has written books for two of the contributors and had some kind of contact with at least five others, I thought I had a decent idea about what was required for different kinds of books aimed at different audiences. But there was much I had not realized. These editors have shepherded into print quickie pamphlets and book series (especially biblical, theological, and ethical) making up small libraries in their own right. They have prepared books for catechism classes, Sunday schools, professional fields, professional sub-fields, professional sub-sub-fields, and the mythical general public. They have gone to bat with their firms' final decision-makers for academic books destined for a minuscule number of readers and transformed more than a few humdrum, ordinary titles into bestsellers. Add in children's books, young adult fiction, reference works of several types, and the attentive reader will come away realizing that "Christian publishing" is as capacious as the amorphous category of "religious books."

Stephanie Derrick's diligence in recruiting far and wide has made for at least one noteworthy contribution that readers might not anticipate. Her contributors have worked not just with white audiences and African Americans in the United States. They have also labored in England, Canada, and at the Vatican; in Brazil and Peru; in South Africa and other African nations; as well as in Pakistan, South Korea, and the Philippines. Since these editors have worked for publishers serving ethnic Protestants, mainline Protestants, white and Black evangelicals, Pentecostals, and Catholics of several varieties, their accounts turn out to introduce the remarkable worldwide reach of contemporary Christianity. If Christian publishing once had a center in the "Christian West," the center is now dispersed to the world.

Readers, in sum, should be prepared for a cornucopia of insight from good writing by veteran editors about the production of Christian books from the germ of an author's idea to a secure place on the backlist—and also a great deal more.

PHILIP YANCEY

Farewell to the Golden Age

I HAVE LIVED THROUGH the golden age of publishing, first with magazines and then with books. I began my career at *Campus Life* in 1971, and in ten years saw our circulation leap from 50,000 to 250,000. Like many magazines, *Campus Life* eventually bit the dust as advertising dollars migrated to flashier (and cheaper) online sources and consumers no longer responded to direct mail offers and renewal letters.

For four decades I've worked as a freelance writer, feeling enormously blessed to make a good living by writing about issues of faith that I would want to explore even if no one bought my books. Every year my royalties decrease, though with twenty books in print I can still pay bills and find publishers willing to sponsor new books.

The changes in publishing, especially Christian publishing, stood out sharply to me when I attended a recent Christian book convention. At one time 15,000 attended that trade show, a convention so large that only a handful of cities could accommodate it. Now only a few thousand attend, and the sponsoring organization is struggling to stay in business.

In truth, many Christian bookstores were "mom and pop" stores run more out of a sense of ministry than business acumen. Managers stocked too many titles, knew little about marketing, and stayed in business mainly because every so often a mega-seller like *The Purpose Driven Life* or the *Left Behind* series would come along to rescue their bottom line. In the early 1990s chain stores such as Walmart, Costco, and Sam's Club started picking off these bestsellers and general bookstores like Borders (now defunct) and Barnes & Noble greatly expanded their religion departments. Then came

Amazon.com, offering deep discounts to siphon off the steady sales that kept small bookstores afloat.

There was a cost to the industry, of course. No longer would shoppers browse the shelves, pick up books to scan the contents, and walk out with five books when they had intended to buy just one. Now they ordered the one they wanted online, untempted by new books they did not even know existed. Scores of college and seminary bookstores closed as students ordered the required books online, forfeiting the ability to browse among unassigned books that also might interest them. One large publisher recently told me they sell 81 percent of their books online (mainly through Amazon, ChristianBook.com, and other such outlets) as opposed to brick-and-mortar stores.

The digital revolution has introduced a whole new challenge to the publishing industry, much like its impact on music and movies. For publishers and also authors (the "plankton" of the publishing food chain), this has meant a drastic reduction in income. Say an author signs a contract to receive a royalty on the net income for each book sold. In the old days he or she would receive $3.00 on a $30 hardback book. Now Amazon offers the book electronically for $14.99 and often offers specials as low as $1.99. For the same amount of work, the author will receive a fraction of the royalties.

Publishers receive reduced income for ebooks as well, but their costs are greatly reduced; it's much cheaper to download a digital file compared to the many steps involved in "dead-tree" publishing. Writers bear the brunt of this price-cutting: surveys by Authors Guild show that income for freelancers has dropped by 30 to 40 percent in the last decade.

For a first-time author, these are the best of times and the worst of times. Thanks to advances in self-publishing, anyone can get a book in print—as long as you're willing to bear the costs of production, marketing, and sales that used to be absorbed by publishers. Brick-and-mortar bookstores generally won't stock your book, so you have to find other ways to get the word out. Good luck.

I had an enlightening experience with ebooks in 2013. In April I finished the book *The Question That Never Goes Away*, based on my visits to three places of great tragedy. My traditional publisher wanted at least nine months lead time to publish it, the typical schedule for a new book, yet new tragedies such as the Boston Marathon bombings, tornadoes, and school shootings were occurring almost weekly, the very situations my book addressed. So I signed on for an Amazon-exclusive program to publish an ebook for ninety days before the hardcopy book came out. Leaning on my friends for email lists, I managed to sell about 3,000 copies. On September 11 and Thanksgiving weekend I offered free downloads and 40,000 people downloaded the book! The moral of the story, as many have learned: things can quickly go viral on the Internet but it's a tough place to generate income.

Trust me, I have no sour grapes. My main motive in writing the book was to bring perspective and comfort to people going through hard times, and if 40,000 people got it free, all the better. As I say, I have made a good living from writing and would probably keep doing it even if all my books were free. I do worry, though, about new authors who don't have a backlist to depend on. As readers are trained to pay less (or nothing) for books, how can authors survive?

There's still hope for traditional publishing. Predictions that ebooks will make print obsolete have proven wrong. Though they have found their niche, the impact on publishing has not followed the streaming pattern of music and movies. Even younger readers still prefer a physical book they can hold, dog-ear, and make notes in.

Some studies show that people read slower on dedicated e-readers, and those who use tablets or computers or smartphones have a different reading experience, being constantly distracted by text messages, emails, Facebook, and other interruptions. Nicholas Carr's *The Shallows: What the Internet Is Doing to Our Brains* explores how the brain copes with these distractions. Hyperlinked, multitasking readers do not have the same "deep reading" experience, and are less likely to store what they read in long-term memory. In Carr's words, "Once I was a scuba diver in the sea of words. Now I zip along the surface like a guy on a Jet Ski."

We are living through a revolution in both reading and publishing not unlike the one Gutenberg introduced almost 700 years ago. Nowadays authors are coached on how to "build your brand" through blogs and podcasts, more than on improving their writing. Publishers seem to care more about website stats and Twitter followers than the quality of an author's work.

Frankly, I'm glad I'm as old as I am. It's been fun living through publishing's golden age. I'll happily stick with the "deep reading" experience. Nothing gives me more satisfaction than browsing through the books in my office. They're my friends—marked up, dog-eared, highlighted, a kind of spiritual and intellectual journal—in a way that my Kindle reader or an audiobook will never be.

STEPHANIE L. DERRICK
_____

Introduction

ON SEPTEMBER 30, 1952, the publication of a new translation of the Bible was met with celebrations by more than 2 million people at meetings and special services in 3,400 communities across the United States and Canada. Of such national interest and importance was Thomas Nelson's new Revised Standard Version that it was widely discussed in American newspapers and, to mark the occasion, officials in Washington, DC issued a commemorative stamp honoring the five hundredth birthday of the Gutenberg Bible.[1] Today the notion that a general public—even one as religious as is found in the United States—would react with such fervor to the publishing of a religious text is hardly imaginable. Indeed, the RSV's reception in 1952 suggests just how much the goings-on of religious publishing—and perhaps religion in general—has receded from mainstream America's cultural spotlight in the decades since.

At this writing in 2020, the entire global publishing industry is facing challenges as a result of the COVID-19 pandemic, and it will undoubtedly evolve in significant ways as a result. At such a critical juncture and with so much unknown about the future, it is a particularly fitting time to present a collection of essays reflecting on Christian publishing since mid-century, decades that witnessed a steady stream of important developments. Indeed, nearly all aspects of the process of connecting the labor of authors with audiences were transformed in this period: from how creative pieces are transmitted, to who walks the halls of publishing houses, to the forces shaping how people decide what to read. *Chasing Paper* offers a series of reflections, therefore, from those who have been witnesses to these

1. Tebbel, *History of Book Publishing*, 595.

developments and key changemakers themselves, about the meaning and importance of these evolutions. While the whole of the publishing industry has changed, Christian publishing is the focus here because there is very little documenting this particular genre. Indeed, the anecdote about the publication of the Revised Standard Version is demonstrative in a second, less obvious way. While Christian publishing has a rich, complicated global history, what scholarship there is available on the subject skews heavily toward the West and the majority concerns the United States. Presently, there are no substantive histories to hand, for example, of twentieth-century Christian publishing in Nigeria, South Africa, Brazil, France, or even Vatican City. This is a subject in need of much more attention.

To that end, *Chasing Paper* collects essays by Christian publishing leaders from various countries and sub-sectors of a diverse industry, all of whom were asked to speak to their own experiences with a changing industry. Through their writings we catch a glimpse of what these gatekeepers of Christian print culture think about a niche, yet important industry. Many speak here to why they are (or were) in publishing to begin with, the challenges these last decades have presented, how their companies navigated those challenges, and what they believe was and is at stake. But why should we care what they have to say? After all, religious publishing is a small slice of publishing overall (e.g. about 5 percent in the US and 2 percent of UK bestsellers) and little noticed by those outside of it.[2] Yet, consider the matter from a broader perspective. Religion is an essential part of human meaning and society; Christianity is the world's largest religion; and Christian publishing, at least until recently, played a critical role in the intellectual culture of the world's Christians by making decisions about what is published. If Christian publishers have historically played a part in what was and was not available to read, then understanding more about their perspectives has implications for wider society indeed. What and who did they deem worthy of attention? What did they see as the ultimate goal for their companies or publishing arms? How did their decisions shape wider opinion? This book will not answer all of these questions, but it does help document a moment and therefore is a step in the right direction.

---

2. See Gutjahr, "Perseverance," 377, and *passim* on the growth of religious publishing in the US and the difficulties of measuring it; and Ledger-Lomas, "Religion," 393, citing Feather and Woodbridge.

CHRISTIAN PUBLISHING AS SUBJECT

As mentioned, one difficulty with Christian publishing as a subject is that the historiography is extremely uneven and marred by Western bias. This introductory overview of Christian publishing and the changes it has undergone in recent years will regrettably, therefore, also be Western and American-centric due to the limitations of the sources. Accounts of religious and Christian publishing are still few, and in fact scholars have only recently delivered sufficient studies on the twentieth and twenty-first century publishing industry in general to provide a picture of the many factors affecting change across various segments. Furthermore, we are still far too close in time to many of the most consequential of these to appraise their implications and significance.

That said, the accounts that are available hint at a strange and interesting ecosystem. Longtime editor of Random House, Jason Epstein, wrote of trade publishing that it "is by nature a cottage industry, decentralized, improvisational, personal; best performed by small groups of like-minded people, devoted to their craft, jealous of their autonomy, sensitive to the needs of writers and to the diverse interests of readers. If money were their primary goal, these people would probably have chosen other careers."[3] This is an apt description of Christian publishing, too, for much of the twentieth century and to some extent even today. It, too, is a world peppered with characters and intense personalities who are intently focused on a higher calling. The *particularity* of Christian publishing revolves around the religious tenor of that calling, and, perhaps, the fervor with which it is held. Christian publishing manifests the tension within all publishing since at least the fifteenth century—that between art and profit—and infuses it with a sense of purpose and language with which the faithful are familiar. Over and over throughout the following essays we hear references to the "mission" and "calling" of Christian publishing. This, I suggest, is one of the most notable features of our subject: the sincerity and frequency with which industry professionals describe their businesses in missional language.

A second striking thing about Christian publishing is that it is its own galaxy within the universe of publishing, with a multitude of sub-worlds that sometimes bump into one another but often do not. To state the obvious, Christian publishing, as I use the term here—that is, in the broadest possible sense and primarily with book publishing in mind—mirrors

3. Epstein, *Book Business,* 1.

mainstream publishing in that it has its own academic, educational, professional, children's, and trade sectors.[4] It also has its own variance of ownership structures: denominational publishing houses serving the needs of the Franciscans, the Brethren, or the Unitarian Universalists; Protestant for-profits competing with one another for their share of the Bible market; non-profits focused on the production of hymnals, biblical commentaries, or evangelistic pamphlets, etc. The iterations are many. Christian publishing is also no different from other sectors of publishing in that it has innovated and adapted in order to survive a rapidly changing world. Consolidation and corporate ownership have affected much of the industry, just as elsewhere. But there still remain many independent actors. Finding creative solutions to the needs of a diverse customer base has been the way that religious publishing has survived, and in some cases thrived, through the early twenty-first century. Because Christian publishing is varied and serves a niche audience, and also because it is closely tied to churches, seminaries, and other religiously affiliated institutions, it has to date resisted becoming *as* monolithic and corporate as trade publishing. Though larger forces have reshaped the industry dramatically, there are still idiosyncrasies to be found, and it is still a world in which relationships and connections matter very much. Jon Pott didn't plan on working in publishing but what became a five-decade-long career began at Eerdmans, above all, he says, because he had friends at the company. And, as witnessed by this book, even in the late nineties a publisher might still decide on a new editorial hire at a company-hosted wine party.[5] So, while much has changed, much has not.

CHRISTIAN PUBLISHING: A SKETCH OF KEY CHANGES SINCE THE MID-TWENTIETH CENTURY

What has changed about Christian publishing from about 1950 to 2020? In a word, for most people working in this sphere the *why* did not change, but almost everything about the *how* did. The following section will provide high level and very brief observations about some of the key changes, to give some context for the essays that follow.

4. For a discussion of definitions see Rubin, "Boundaries," 207–17.

5. Pott, "Two Worlds," 117; Stock, "Early Days," 142.

TECHNOLOGICAL CHANGES

As is often observed, the twentieth and early twenty-first centuries witnessed rapid technological development. In the 1970s and eighties, typesetters applied computers and software to the composition of books and lowered the cost to publishers. From the mid-eighties desktop publishing and word-processing programs began to be adopted. Simultaneously, communication technology advances increased the speed of communication. As Greg Thornton writes, "Connecting with others has advanced from hand-typed memos on an electric typewriter, to dictating letters on recorders with mini cassette tapes, to desktop computers connected to printers with faxing capability, to computers with Internet bringing email to life, to texting, to Twitter. Still there's always been the phone."[6] In 2007 Apple released the iPhone and Amazon launched their Kindle electronic book reader; 2010 saw the release of the iPad for purchasing ebooks. The inventions of the personal computer, the Internet, and ebooks have been among the most consequential advances across all of book publishing, including Christian publishing. As Peter Dwyer observed in his essay, "Overnight e-book formats, digital rights, and the shockingly low ebook prices that Amazon introduced to fuel growth in Kindle sales became the new obsession."[7] By 2011 Amazon announced that sales of ebooks had surpassed print sales in the USA.[8] Digital printing had enabled, among other things, publishers to print much smaller print runs and thus reduce the need for storage of back stock and react more nimbly to market demands. To these developments were added an increased use in recent years of audiobooks, supported by advances in mobile phone technologies.

CHANGES IN BUSINESS PRACTICES AND RETAIL

Technological advances were a critical driver of change across publishing but so, too, were evolving business models and practices. Since as far back as the fifteenth century, with many factors enabling its expansion, publishing has marched forward on a continuum of increasingly more sophisticated business structures and organization. In the twentieth century this trajectory accelerated and the industry became much more professionalized:

6. Thornton, "Glorious Deeds," 146.

7. Dwyer, "Six Decades," 74.

8 Clark and Phillips, *Inside Book Publishing*, 15.

publishers became more focused on the management and production of content, while the role of the literary agent evolved to represent authors' interests. Beginning in the sixties, and especially from the late eighties, "in order to grow effectively and satisfy shareholders with increasing profits, there was a trend towards more mergers and acquisitions in order to develop market 'clout' and gain market share."[9] This meant, at minimum, that a number of Christian publishing companies were bought by larger publishing companies. Perhaps the Christian publishing sector was an especially attractive investment because religious books, at least in the United States, were growing at a faster rate than other genres. In 1979 they composed only 5 percent of the 40,000 new books issued, but in terms of growth rate they were far ahead of other segments of the business, recording 112 percent from 1972 to 1977 while the industry as a whole was growing at 70 percent.[10] The trend of mergers and acquisitions continued through the early twenty-first century. In 2020 many independent companies remain, but the rise of multimedia conglomerations and their involvement in publishing has greatly altered the publishing landscape. Since 2011 HarperCollins, for example, has controlled about half of the Christian publishing market in America.[11]

Tied to this development were major changes to the way Christian publishers reached their customers. For much of the twentieth century, one of the key differences between Christian publishing and other sectors was that the former operated largely outside the book trade mainstream, with specialist bookstores and direct mail to religious book club members and churches being heavily relied upon for sales.[12] Such practices insulated Christian publishers, for a time and to some extent, from turbulent markets and corporate buyouts. As Joseph Sinasac discusses in his essay, direct distribution methods have continued to be a stabilizing factor for Catholic publisher Novalis, as it has been for others.[13]

The challenges posed by Amazon, however, have changed the industry and—together with other complex forces—resulted in the closing of thousands of Christian bookstores in recent years. As Simone Murray has put it, "Since Amazon's founding in 1994, the whole way in which books are

9. Hall, "Organizational Structures in Publishing," 293.

10. Tebbel, *History of Book Publishing*, 589.

11. Olsen, "HarperCollins Buys Thomas Nelson."

12. Tebbel, *History of Book Publishing*, 589

13. Sinasac, "From the Great Depression," 52–54.

created, marketed, publicized, sold, reviewed, showcased, consumed, and commented upon has changed dramatically." [14] Indeed, as Jeffrey Wright observes in his essay, "[Christian publishers] faced a different kind of social transformation when Amazon became the number one seller of books, leading to the near demise of an entire industry of Christian book and retail stores." [15] Peter Dwyer also elucidates the forces at work and one Catholic publisher's response:

> Small independent booksellers were especially hard hit, including religious bookstores. But many religious-owned publishers also have direct-to-customer (consumer and institutional) sales that were undercut by Amazon's loss-leader discounting. Increased discoverability for backlist in the Amazon ecosystem was touted as an offset to the loss of margin. The reality is that after all costs of doing business with Amazon are counted, it is an unprofitable re-lationship for many publishers . . . To protect our direct business as Amazon grew, [Liturgical Press] began in the late 1990s to develop annual books designed for bulk sales to parishes—a difficult trans-action for Amazon and other online resellers. Though Amazon's share of our book sales continues to rise, the annuals are almost entirely direct-to-customer and now account for 10 percent of our book revenue. [16]

The rise of Amazon, together with all of the technologies that enabled it, paired with the demise of independent retail outlets and the trend toward corporate buy-outs has entirely changed much of the way Christian pub-lishers do business.

AN ALTERED PUBLISHING CULTURE

As Christian retail outlets closed and Amazon's share of book sales in-creased, as the industry has became more globalized, professionalized, technologically sophisticated, and business savvy, Christian publishing has had to adapt to survive. From the top to the bottom, all around the world, all aspects of Christian book publishing have been affected because the parts are connected. The closing of retail outlets has changed marketing tactics, which has affected authors. As literary agent Blythe Daniel observed

14. Murray, *Digital Literary Sphere,* book description.
15. Wright, "Publishing African American Christians," 67.
16. Dwyer, "Six Decades," 73–74.

in 2019, "the shrinking footprint of Christian retailers is already leading to a new normal where writers are also expected to have a marketing team behind them."[17] Indeed, in 2020, because much of the responsibility of publicity has shifted to the author, especially when they are yet to be established, an author's social media presence and influence online is an important factor that publishers consider when deciding whether to publish their book. This fact alone has profound consequences for *who* and *what* is published. In such conditions known authors are likely to be favored and new voices are less likely to be let in the door.

Furthermore, within publishing companies themselves, *who* holds power has shifted. Even the language used to describe what publishing is about has been altered: as Robin Baird-Smith describes it, "Books came to be known so poetically as 'product' and selling books became known as 'the through put of units.' Salesmen and accountants were in the ascendant and the so called 'creative' departments were in decline. The power of the editor waned."[18] More and more print content has been produced in recent years—because new technologies have allowed it to be done more economically—but that content must compete against a greater overall volume of print media than in past years, as well as with an increasingly screen-focused culture and a plethora of other forms of entertainment like movies, television, and podcasts. On the one hand, there has been an expansion of titles[19] but in reality "more books [are] being read by fewer people."[20]

Looking at the last twenty years, especially, of Christian publishing, there is a sense of things *thinning out*, as if the industry has been stretched to the limit. The situation is brimming with paradoxes. More books are being published each year but few of the well-established publishers now will consider an unsolicited manuscript. It is harder to break in as an author but also easier to go around the industry entirely and self-publish. There are many more women working in publishing today but few are given the publisher title and in any case that title means less now than it did twenty years ago. Today, denominational identity is something less closely held than it was in the past by Western Christians but there are publishing companies surviving because of its continuing salience in some communities. There has been enormous change in Christian publishing but, still, family-owned

---

17. As summarized by Ann Byle, "Agents Discuss the New Norms," lines 17–18.
18. Baird-Smith, "Religious Book Publishing," 57.
19. Le Peau, "Evangelical Academic Book Publishing," 97, 105.
20. Carpenter, "The Changing Face," 8.

companies like R. H. Boyd Company, Eerdmans, and others have had long-lived editors and publishers who have provided continuity and leadership through turbulent decades.

CONCLUSION: CHANGE IS NOT NEUTRAL

While developments in technology and evolving business practices certainly are among the most consequential of developments in publishing, the devil is in the details when it comes to understanding both the scale of change, as well as the degree of consistency, in Christian publishing. And detail is what this field is lacking. Indeed, the existing scholarly literature on publishing in general only scratches the surface of a complicated affair. As scholar Elizabeth le Roux rightly observed, when it comes to publishing studies:

> the focus on increasing commercialization and commodification, and on the impact of technology, demonstrates a step back from engaging with issues of the social and, especially, of the political. Do we still see a social and political role for the publishing industry in the twenty-first century? Are we still interrogating the links between publishing and ideology? There is a great deal of scope for further research that engages directly with the social role of publishing, and that recognizes its political dimensions.[21]

I couldn't agree more. Exploring the social and political role of Christian publishing in particular seems to me an important undertaking. However, in order to do that we need more details and documentation, which is one way this book makes a contribution.

When we are enabled to look more closely, the results can be surprising. Peter Dwyer, for example, shows us that sometimes innovation in response to change can be counterintuitive, such as the success of *Give Us This Daily*, a "monthly print publication that supports the practice of daily prayer." Liturgical Press began publication of it in 2011 and "eight years later it has circulation of 100,000 and climbing" and "accounts for one-third of Liturgical Press revenue."[22] Likewise, it was not at all obvious that InterVarsity Press would have the success that they did in the 1990s with academic titles: evidence that change in this sphere is far from a linear,

21. Le Roux, "Publishing and Society," 95.

22. Dwyer, "Six Decades," 77.

predictable affair.[23] Even denominational affiliations are less predictable than one might imagine, with evangelical publishers like Baker and Eerdmans moving into the Catholic theological book market in the early twenty-first century.[24]

Christian publishing is an industry driven by human decisions as much as it is by larger social, economic, and technological forces, and this book is an opportunity to hear the reasons behind the launch of a new series or why a publisher took a more ecumenical turn. Furthermore, as Roy Carlisle and others remind us, cultural context, too, is very much a determinate, for example, as in the case of books retaining much prestige in Brazil or Peru or the profound effects of theological decisions made by the Second Vatican Council. While recent work on the publishing industry in general is making it clearer what the broader trends have been, we have much more work to do on the profound social, political, even spiritual, implications of changes in religious publishing. This is especially true when it comes to the situation outside North America and Europe.

What is clear to me is that when it comes to arbitrating culture, as publishers do, in an environment that is morphing at great speed, as has been the case over the last twenty years in particular, change is not neutral. There are gains and losses that are difficult to identify and even harder to quantify. For example, what is the psychological or social consequence of what Robert Hudson identifies as "the increasing mechanization of the publishing process, the tendency to view bookmaking as an assembly line rather than a craft"? Or consider the conclusion Mickey Maudlin came to about the books (and thus culture and companies) that reward individualism, sensationalism, and consumerism. Maudlin wrote:

> Eventually the scales fell off and I had to confront the uncomfortable truth that perhaps evangelical churches, books, personalities and programs were the most popular because the movement was the most accommodated to consumer culture. Seeing evangelicalism as a populist movement, subject to fads and personality cults, fit with many of the dynamics I witnessed. I certainly don't want to imply that is all evangelicalism is (one must leave room for the Holy Spirit), but this goes a long way to explain why evangelicals seem to have all the Christian bestsellers.[25]

23. Le Peau, "Evangelical Academic Book Publishing," passim.

24. Le Peau, "Evangelical Academic Book Publishing," 100.

25. Maudlin, "Why Evangelicals," lines 17–23.

Such an observation deserves further exploration and especially as it pertains to how such patterns affect reader behavior.[26] Who has been pushed to the margins and what thoughts have not met with a printing press because they did not promise quick, big sales or because publishers would not risk offending the owners of Christian bookstore chains or their customers?[27] And what of the loss of many local bookstores themselves, access to conversations with the kinds of individuals who run them, and the experience of browsing shelves? And what is the consequence of deciding what to read based on recommendations produced by an algorithm created by Amazon or Google? How might Pieter Kwant's life as a reader, a publisher, and a person of insight been different had he not encountered the NG Kerkboekhandel bookstore in South Africa?[28] For that matter, a few of the essayists describe how a love of books they had as children led to careers in publishing. Are we right, those of us who assume that such a love will inevitably be passed down to future generations, or are we taking some things for granted? As noted by several in this book, the way we read is itself changing and fewer people are choosing to write full time due to the difficulty of making a living doing so.[29] That is not to say the situation in Christian publishing or publishing in general is necessarily worse than in, say, 1980. New technologies have enabled readers and publishers to discover voices that were routinely silenced in decades past and who would want that development reversed? Still, change, in the case of Christian publishing, is not neutral.

It is my hope that this book inspires more scholars to shed light on Christian publishing in all of its varieties and in all the places it is found and that it inspires those working in the publishing industry to further observe, document, and discuss, their fascinating and important mission of words.

26. Daniel Vaca has addressed the relationship between evangelicalism and consumerism in *Evangelicals Incorporated*.

27. E.g., the books of Jen Hatmaker were pulled by Lifeway over her support of same-sex marriage. See Shellnutt, "The Bigger Story."

28. Kwant, "We Are," 10–12.

29. On how reading is changing see: Yancey, "Farewell," xiii; Hudson, "Of Octavos and Octothorpes," passim; Baird-Smith, "Religious Book Publishing," 57–61. On the decline of professional authors see Larson, "Authors Guild Issues Report."

BIBLIOGRAPHY

Byle, Ann. "Agents Discuss the New Norms of Christian Publishing." *Publishers Weekly*, May 8, 2019. https://www.publishersweekly.com/pw/by-topic/industry-news/religion/article/79976-agents-discuss-the-new-norms-of-christian-publishing.html.

Clark, Giles, and Angus Phillips. *Inside Book Publishing*. 6th ed. New York: Routledge, 2020.

Epstein, Jason. *Book Business: Publishing Past Present and Future*. New York: W. W. Norton & Company, 2002.

Feather, John, and Hazel Woodbridge. "Bestsellers in the British Book Industry 1998–2005." *Publishing Research Quarterly* 23 (2007) 210–23.

Gutjahr, Paul C. "The Perseverance of Print-Bound Saints: Protestant Book Publishing." In *A History of the Book in America*, vol. 5, edited by David Paul Nord, Joan Shelley Rubin, and Michael Schudson, 376–88. Chapel Hill, NC: University of North Carolina Press, 2009.

Hall, Frania. "Organizational Structures in Publishing." In *The Oxford Handbook of Publishing*, edited by Angus Phillips and Michael Bhaskar, 291–309. Oxford: Oxford University Press, 2019.

Larson, Christine. "Authors Guild Issues Report Exploring the Factors Leading to the Decline of the Writing Profession." February 19, 2020. https://www.authorsguild.org/industry-advocacy/authors-guild-issues-report-exploring-the-factors-leading-to-the-decline-of-the-writing-profession/.

Le Roux, Elizabeth. "Publishing and Society." In *The Oxford Handbook of Publishing*, edited by Angus Phillips and Michael Bhaskar, 85–98. Oxford: Oxford University Press, 2019.

Ledger-Lomas, Michael. "Religion." In *The Cambridge History of the Book in Britain: Vol VII, The Twentieth Century and Beyond*, edited by Andrew Nash, Claire Squires, and I. R. Willison, 392–426. Cambridge: Cambridge University Press, 2019.

Maudlin, Mickey. "Why Evangelicals Have All the Bestsellers." *Huffington Post*, February 19, 2013. https://www.huffpost.com/entry/why-evangelicals-have-all-the-bestsellers_b_2679131.

Murray, Simone. *The Digital Literary Sphere: Reading, Writing and Selling Books in the Internet Era*. Baltimore: Johns Hopkins University Press, 2020.

Olsen, Ted. "HarperCollins Buys Thomas Nelson, Will Control 50% of Christian Publishing Market." *Christianity Today*, October 31, 2011. https://www.christianitytoday.com/news/2011/october/harpercollins-buys-thomas-nelson-will-control-50-of.html.

Rubin, Joan Shelley. "The Boundaries of American Religious Publishing," *Book History* 2 (1999) 207–17.

Shellnutt, Kate. "The Bigger Story Behind Jen Hatmaker." *Christianity Today*, November 15, 2016. https://www.christianitytoday.com/ct/2016/november-web-only/bigger-story-behind-jen-hatmaker.html

Tebbel, John R. *A History of Book Publishing in the United States*, vol. 4, *The Great Change, 1940–1980*. New York: R. R. Bowker, 1981.

Vaca, Daniel. *Evangelicals Incorporated: Books and the Business of Religion in America*. Cambridge, MA: Harvard University Press, 2019.

MARK CARPENTER

The Changing Face of Publishing
in Brazil

AUGUST 8, 2010. AN impatient crowd packed the multilevel Cultura bookstore in downtown São Paulo. Most of them hovered around a roped-off
table. Tonight a book signing was scheduled. As the publisher of this new
book, I waited to greet the writer and open the event. The book was a biography of Marina Silva, the world-renowned environmentalist, presidential
candidate, and outspoken Christian. The author of the authorized biography was to be accompanied by Marina herself, and together they would
sign copies for the crowd. Mixed among Marina's fans were nationally-
known politicians, pundits, and culture-makers. Marina appeared through
a side door and headed for the table. Her slight, fragile figure was dressed
as always, in organic textiles and adorned with an elegant seed necklace
handmade by an indigenous artisan. News photographers and TV camera-
men scrambled for the best shot. The crowd jockeyed into position to form
a line, get their books signed, and take selfies with Marina.

As I moved into the shadows with some of my staff, I realized that this
moment symbolized a culmination of our long-held dreams. For decades
our publishing house had worked to improve the quality of our books and
set new standards for Christian publishing in Brazil. We had done our best
to break into the country's secular book-distribution network, develop the
press-relations network needed to have our authors featured in the country's
top media, and shift away from a steady diet of translated books to publish
books written locally. The ultimate goal: to curate and amplify voices that

1

influence the church and Brazilian society for the cause of Christ, propelling the best Christian books into the public eye.

As the young son of American missionaries growing up in a small town in Brazil's interior in the 1960s and '70s, I often felt stuck. Not stuck in Brazil, but isolated from the world at large. Our small town had four AM radio stations, one TV channel, and one daily newspaper. I attended a tiny school for American missionary kids. Its library was understocked and weighted toward aging textbooks and Young Adult fiction. My father's personal library was more erudite, but was comprised mostly of theological books. Each night after dinner he gathered my brothers and me to listen to him read books such as the Narnia series. He stirred in me a love of books and a deep interest in knowledge about the outside world.

Occasionally he would get new books in English or Portuguese. I couldn't help but notice the difference between his American and Brazilian books. Most imported volumes were produced with an intentionality that exuded an adherence to standards. The paper, suited for high-resolution type, seemed to lend the authority of perfection to the words of the authors. My father taught me how to handle these books. How to remove a dust jacket while reading. How to break in a new hardcover by bending back each signature so as not to crack the binding. How to hold the volume while taking it from the shelf or putting it back. In contrast, the Christian books produced in Brazil were amateurish. Many had plastic-coated covers that would bend and warp away from the book blocks. They failed to measure up even to the standards set by the best Brazilian secular publishing houses. Most of these Christian books were translations of works by American or European authors. The few original works by local authors were poorly edited and thus difficult to read.

The missionary school I attended used a US-based curriculum. Brazilian teachers were brought in to supplement our education by providing classes in the Portuguese language and Brazilian literature, history, and geography. It was in these classes that I first became interested in the culture of Brazil. Outside of class I became friends with many Brazilians—my neighbors, youth group acquaintances, and friends of their friends. My desire to fit in led me to an appreciation of all things Brazil, including its history of immigration and its forms of artistic and cultural expression. I spent time at the municipal library, the record store, and the Banca do Massao, an unusually well-stocked newsstand that sold the country's best literary, political, and cultural magazines. Through voices of dissent in journalism, poetry, and protest songs, I became aware of the devastating effects of the military dictatorship then in power and the struggle to reclaim democracy. I wanted to be a part of this story. At some point in the early 1970s, during my high school years, I decided that I wanted to spend the rest of my life in Brazil.

I moved to the US for university studies. There I discovered a wealth of periodical literature in college libraries and bookstores. I became aware of the scope and power of good writing to change minds and lives, and decided that the world of literature is where I wanted to spend my career. I worked at two magazines, then went to work for Tyndale House (Wheaton, Illinois) as a book editor. As I learned the trade, Brazil was never far from my mind. Then I received a job offer from Mundo Cristão, a Christian publisher in São Paulo.

I arrived in Brazil in 1985 with my wife, Laurie. Mundo Cristão was small but well-organized. It published a translation of the *Living Bible* and a steady stream of books. The market was growing quickly as the evangelical church continued to expand. The evangelical market was served by several publishers in addition to Mundo Cristão:

- The Brazilian Bible Society, founded in 1948, which distributes the most popular Bible translation, the Almeida.

- CPAD, an Assemblies of God publisher producing books and Christian education material for use by the denomination.

- Vida, owned by the missions division of the U.S. Assemblies of God

- Betânia, linked to Bethany Fellowship USA.

- Vida Nova, a Conservative Baptist academic and reference book publisher.

- JUERP, the publishing arm of the Brazilian Baptist Convention.

- Several smaller houses, mostly linked to denominations or parachurch ministries.

Many of the personnel lacked experience in management or skill in the field. In 1988 these publishing houses collectively founded ASEC, an association of Christian publishers whose goals included training, liaising with book-related trade associations, and providing a forum for networking.

Most publishers produced Bibles and translations of nonfiction from publishers such as Zondervan, Tyndale, Harvest House, Gospel Light,

Eerdmans, Baker, Crossway, Bethany, Thomas Nelson, and others. Their products were sold to wholesalers such as Milenium, Christian Literature Crusade, Socep, and the wholesale divisions of CPAD, Vida, and Betânia. These in turn sold books to smaller commercial bookstores, church shops, and colporteurs. There was no market for Christian books in secular bookstore chains such as Siciliano, Saraiva, Brasiliense, or LaSelva. Attempts made by Christian sales staff were often met with arguments that their readers would not be interested in religious books with little appeal to the general public.

THEN AND NOW

Much has changed over the past forty years in Christian publishing in Brazil. Many of the changes reflect the deep shifts occurring in book publishing worldwide, such as the introduction of ebooks, the popularization of audiobooks, the change in the way readers discover and buy books, the new financial viability of short print runs and print on demand, and the rise of new technologies competing for the time of those who used to rely on reading for information and entertainment. But other changes are unique to Brazil because of the expansion and influence of the church, the nature of local political and economic crises, the acute polarization of Christians into theological and political camps, and the perceived value of books amid the quickly expanding panorama of content options.

Cost of entry

In the early 1980s the capital requirements for breaking into the market as a new publisher were relatively high. The costs of typesetting, printing, and binding were significant, and the need for reserving funds for reprints took a heavier toll on cash-flow planning. Thus, the largest eight evangelical publishing houses dominated the market and another twelve or so competed for the remaining share. Today the cost of entry has been dramatically reduced. Technology allows any individual to write, edit, typeset, and design a book, and then make it available in ebook or print format to anyone on the Internet. Established publishing houses now face more competitors, including well-known authors enticed with the prospect of keeping a larger portion of the revenues generated by sales of the books they produce themselves. Traditional publishers now need to work harder than

4

ever to carefully curate their catalogs, demonstrate the editorial superiority of books produced by professionals, and market their products nationwide as trustworthy, relevant, and compelling.

Market size and new players

In the early 1980s, approximately 8 percent of the Brazilian population was evangelical. During subsequent decades this percentage has grown exponentially, and today stands at nearly 30 percent. This evolving market has attracted the attention of other publishing houses. In 2006 Thomas Nelson set up a Brazilian division. International publishing conglomerates such as Spain's Planeta have set up local imprints specializing in Christian books, and Brazilian trade and literary houses such as Sextante and Globo have begun publishing evangelical authors.

Discoverability of new releases and bestsellers

In the past, readers found books by visiting the local Christian bookstore and browsing the shelves and new-release tables. In subsequent years, due to the growth of the Christian population, secular stores also began stocking books by evangelical publishers. Evangelical books, now more well designed and produced—many indistinguishable in production quality from the best of the secular trade—began to be sold side by side with self-help books and secular bestsellers. In 2014 the Brazilian economy slowed and entered a recession from which it has still not fully recovered. The downturn exposed management flaws in Christian bookstores and in some of the largest secular bookstore chains. In 2018 and 2019 several prominent vendors of Christian books closed their doors. The Saraiva and Cultura secular chains—Brazil's largest—sought bankruptcy protection, plunging the publishing sector into a liquidity crisis. As the venues for book buying were reduced, readers had no choice but to shift their buying habits online. Amazon reaped the benefits, as did their locally based online competitors such as Magalu (owned by retailer Magazine Luiza, founded in 1957) and Americanas (part of Lojas Americanas, a nationwide retail conglomerate founded in 1929). Today publishers are scrambling to replace the discoverability models of the past, investing in social media, online partnerships, podcasts, newsletters, and proprietary e-commerce sites to engage and sell to readers directly.

Book reading as a smaller fraction of entertainment/ information universe

The Internet and its evolving mobile portals are facilitating access to the sorts of information and entertainment options that once required movie tickets, magazine and newspaper subscriptions, trips to the library and bookstore, museum visits, admittance to lecture series, concert and theater tickets, church attendance, and other cultural and educational experiences where one's physical presence was required. Even in the best of times, the percentage of Brazilians who regularly acquired and read books was one of the lowest in South America. Today the images, sound bites, texting and social media platforms, and YouTube videos available on even the cheapest smartphones are reducing the number of long-form readers even more. The challenge facing publishers all over the world is most daunting in countries such as Brazil where book reading is sometimes seen as "antisocial."[1] In recent years publishers have had to work doubly hard to market not only their books, but the advantages of book-reading itself.

Local authors

In the 1960s and seventies, as the evangelical church was beginning to take root and grow, many of the denominational and independent seminaries and Bible institutes hired American or British missionaries as professors. Most of these used translations of academic and reference books as their base texts. As a result, the first generations of Brazilian pastors and de-nominational leaders leaned heavily on the writings of foreigners. As the church grew, so did the appetite for the perceived wisdom from overseas. In the 1980s and nineties, as the evangelical population continued to grow, American denominations began to call back or redeploy their mission-aries from Brazil, declaring the country a success story in modern missions and leaving the church to national leadership. Thoroughly Brazilian denominations were planted. The theology and informal liturgy of older denominations began to acculturate in response to local needs and shifting interpretations. This new national identity opened the way for writing by local writers. Mundo Cristão led the way in publishing local authors us-ing the same editorial and production standards present in the best titles from overseas. Editors were identified and trained, and writers soon found

1. Kottak, *Assault on Paradise*, 178.

6

they had the resources and guidance they needed. Today some of the best-selling Christian books in Brazil are written locally, by authors such as Ed René Kivitz, Tiago Brunet, Augustus Nicodemus, Antonio Carlos Costa, and Hernandes Dias Lopes. Publishers are thus actively influencing the direction of the church in Brazil as locally written books on theology, doctrine, and Christian living are used as a basis for organizing courses and conferences and for setting church policy.

New Bible translations

The Brazilian equivalent of the King James Version is the João Ferreira de Almeida translation, completed in the eighteenth century. Translated from the original languages by a Portuguese missionary to Indonesia, this traditional Textus Receptus translation has undergone many changes and revisions. It is used throughout the Portuguese-speaking world in its many variations, some archaic, others revised into contemporary Portuguese and even changed to include twentieth-century New Testament textual criticism. The most popular editions of the Almeida in Brazil are the *Corrigida*, the *Corrigida Fiel*, the *Revista e Atualizada*, the *Nova Almeida Atualizada*, and the *Almeida Século 21*. These comprise more than 80 percent of the Bible market within Protestant/evangelical circles. Other translations more recently introduced include the NIV-like *Nova Versão Internacional*, the *Nova Bíblia Viva* and *Nova Tradução na Linguagem de Hoje* paraphrases, and the NLT-like *Nova Versão Transformadora*. Until recently, approximately ten million Bibles per year were sold. As free Bible apps such as YouVersion, JFA, and BibliaPlus have been released in recent years, many readers have begun to shift from print to online Scriptures. Publishers have not found ways to monetize online distribution of the Bible, and the revenue stream from Bible sales in the past has begun to decline. Some publishers are focusing on special editions not available on the free apps, such as study and devotional Bibles and editions dedicated to special causes or specific demographics. Others are relying more on fundraising aimed at producing giveaway or heavily subsidized Bibles for distribution to low-income populations.

FROM CRISIS TO CRISIS

The population of Brazil has had to endure many hardships over the past half-century, including the human-rights violations of the military dictatorship that lasted until 1985, the hyperinflation of the 1980s and early nineties, growing income inequality, the deep recession that began in 2014, the disastrous economic and political effects of the Dilma Rousseff administration of the mid 2010s, and the divisive policies of the extreme right-wing Bolsonaro government of recent years, which has polarized the Christian population. The ongoing recession, coupled with the changes in consumer habits due to the development of e-commerce and the expanding popularity of mobile communication and entertainment, exacted a toll on the traditional bookselling sector. In 2019, two of the country's largest bookstore chains sought bankruptcy protection and refused to pay their creditors (mostly publishers) hundreds of millions of Brazilian *reais*. Other chains followed suit, including the largest independent Christian chain, Luz e Vida. In 2020, just as the surviving publishers were finding new ways to cut costs and finance losses, the coronavirus pandemic hit. Suddenly and shockingly, the playing field was leveled for publishers and booksellers across the globe. Some will not survive. Those who do rise from the ashes will need to decide what to recover from the past and what to completely reinvent.

Despite the fragmentation of the publishing process into new suppliers and formats, the book continues to enjoy significant respectability in Brazil, particularly when produced by a credible organization or author. Although the number of books read has slightly declined in the last decade, the number of new titles has grown disproportionately. Thus, we have more books being read by fewer people. Even in this scenario, books still command the attention of journalists, conference organizers, and academia. As one evaluates the nature of the church in Brazil and the scope of its influence, many recent trends and emphases can be traced back to books and authors whose ideas have served as the basis for church policy and who have ignited popular imagination.

What is next? The global economic crisis spawned by the coronavirus pandemic will change the way books are produced, distributed, discovered, and consumed. One thing seems certain: the center focus of our work will never stray far from the compelling voices of the best authors. We will all need leaders, thinkers, and writers to help us make sense of the present and plan for the future. As in the past, some of the most influential minds will communicate truth through long-form, sustained manuscripts that form the foundations for the theories that affect policy. The best authors will help us document our advancing history, distill wisdom from the discoveries of the moment, and suggest paths for progress and meaning amid changing landscapes. Their books will continue to shape our collective consciousness, in Brazil and beyond, and this dynamic ensures the survival of the publishing enterprise in whatever forms may yet emerge.

BIBLIOGRAPHY

Kottak, Conrad Phillip. *Assault on Paradise: The Globalization of a Little Community in Brazil*. New York: McGraw-Hill, 2005.

PIETER KWANT

We Are What We Read: Critical
Reflections on Christian Books and
Publishing in Sub-Saharan Africa

THIS ESSAY HAS TO be my personal story as I am neither an academic nor a researcher. It begins in 1972, when I arrived in South Africa from the Netherlands hoping to start a new chapter in my life. When I met Jesus a few months later in what was then known as the Invisible Church, this "new chapter" became a new life.

Then in 1973 I had what I can only term a baptismal experience with books. A sugar farmer and Baptist lay preacher had invited me to stay with him and do some Bible study. Standing in front of his bookcase early one morning, I picked out *Evangelicalism in England*, by E. J. Poole-Connor. I read it all, and then picked up the book next to it: *George Whitefield*, by John Pollock. I read that from cover to cover too, and then *Revival in Indonesia*, by Kurt Koch, which I read on my knees, as by that time I felt I was on holy ground. In the days that followed I read *The Dust of Death* by Os Guinness and then all the books of Francis Schaeffer. I could not stop . . . the Christian "world" opened up for me, and I realized I was part of a far bigger story. I wanted to know more, much more.

In 1974 I found myself working for NG Kerkboekhandel, a very large theological bookshop in Pretoria, South Africa.[1] I started in the back of-

1. The NG Kerkboekhandel and the NG Kerk Uitgewers were separate organizations serving the same NG Kerk (Church), in the Transvaal and the Cape respectively. On the official material, like the hymnbook for the churches, they were told to work together by the church, but in practice the brotherly relationship was a bit more bristly. The NG

fice, marking books with the selling price, cost price, and original currency selling price. The man working alongside me had a degree in theology, and so we discussed theology, day in and day out, as we marked the prices on books. The customers I met on the shop floor were mostly professors from the University of South Africa (UNISA) and the University of Pretoria (serving both the *Nederduitsch Hervormde Kerk van Afrika* and the *Nederduitsch Gereformeerde Kerk*). They included scholars like Adrio König, Albert Heyns, and David Bosch. I listened to them arguing with each other about the merits of Jürgen Moltmann, Wolfhart Pannenberg, and the like, and was from time to time able to ask them questions as I pointed out books they might be interested in. These interactions became my theological education.

With over 100,000 theological titles in stock in at least seven languages, this shop was an ideal starting ground for a young theological sponge like me! I read many books and skimmed all that came into my hands, whether in English, Dutch, German, French, or Afrikaans. And as I read and skimmed, God started a fire in my heart that is still burning to this day. With my reading and my interactions with customers, I was able to become ever more helpful to them in knowing what they needed to read next. I came to know them and their libraries.

NG Kerkboekhandel operated a well-designed ordering system. It had some 5,000 subscribers who received portions of works like Gerhard Johannes Botterweck's *Theological Dictionary of the Old Testament*, Helmer Ringgren's *Theological Dictionary of the Old Testament*, and Gerhard Kittel's *Theological Dictionary of the New Testament* as they were published. Each volume of the series was distributed in ten parts, and along with the final part, the subscribers would receive the binding so that all the parts could be bound into one book. Subscriptions to these multivolume works were lucrative for both bookshops and publishers and financed the very capital-intensive projects.

The sale of prescribed and recommended books for university courses was also an important part of the business. Professors would set up an appointment with the boss, Mr. Van Straaten (a living theological encyclopedia). They would discuss what books would be needed and in what quantity, and we would then order the books. I well remember the excitement when

---

Kerkboekhandel had the best theological bookshop in the Southern Hemisphere and the NG Kerk Uitgewers concentrated their efforts on more general Christian book trading. The Cape NG Kerk Uitgevers became Lux Verbi in the early 1980s. By that time it had morphed into many bookshops alongside their publishing activities.

the students came in and walked out with piles of between thirty and fifty books each, and sometimes more. We were serving three major universities, so there were hundreds of students. Many of them would come back at regular intervals, requiring ever more books.

The shop also had a specialist ordering and search system for rare and out-of-print books. We kept orders on file for years, sometimes only managing to find a book more than ten years after the order was placed. Our customers were always grateful and surprised. Remember, this was in the seventies, before major search engines took the world by storm. All our research was done by scouring hard-copy catalogues sent by hundreds of secondhand shops and collectors.

It was in that shop that academic bookselling entered my bloodstream. So much so that when the opportunity arose to start my own business in 1978, I eagerly set up as the South African distributor and importer for reformed and evangelical publishers like InterVarsity Press, Banner of Truth, Evangelical Press, and P&R Publishing. I visited many bookshops around the country, both large and small, and got to know other sides of the bookselling trade. As markets changed, I increasingly relied on mail-order sales and on colporteurs to sell on my behalf in the universities.

In 1985 the political situation in South Africa changed dramatically after P. W. Botha delivered his Rubicon speech. The day after the speech, all my capital was wiped off my balance sheet as the South African rand plummeted. International boycotts added to the pressure on the book trade. My selling prices would change every day as I fed new exchange rates into my spreadsheets. It was the only way to survive in a climate that wiped out many other bookshops that could not respond as quickly.

After regaining much of my capital, I eventually sold my business in 1986 and applied to study theology in the Netherlands. But things did not work out as planned, and a year later I started working as the international sales executive for IVP in the UK. During my four years in this job, I travelled the world. It opened my eyes to the global publishing scene.

As I traveled through Africa, I came to realize that Africa was a lot bigger than South Africa! I connected with publishers and distributors in Kenya, Ghana, Nigeria, Uganda, Botswana, Zambia, and Zimbabwe. I, like other evangelical publishers, tried to "help" them by supplying them with cheaper books, remainders, and the like to provide what we thought they needed. What we failed to realize was that by doing this we were making it almost impossible for the few indigenous (mostly popular) publishers to

12

survive. Academic sales through African distributors also shrank as more and more customers obtained their books at yearly Western-organized conferences, cutting out the African middlemen.

From the West to the Rest was our paradigm. Our marketing strategy was that "What comes from the West is best." But in reality, we were sending Africa second-hand books, cast-offs, remainders, and add-on print runs that were cheap for us and "helped them." All done from the best of charitable motives. We had too much, we printed too much, and they needed books (any books), so we gave them the crumbs from our tables.

The paradigm we were using has had very serious consequences for African churches. The assumption that the West is best made Christianity a foreign import. African concerns and questions were never dealt with in the books we provided, and so many of those who read them saw no need to think through African issues as African Christians. A dualistic approach became the norm.

It is said that Africa gets into your heart and under your skin, and so it was with me. During my time at IVP and later as the managing director of Paternoster Press, I never tired of finding ways to "help" Africa. I published two special series of classic theological books especially with Africa in mind. Then after eight years with Paternoster, I resigned. While I was looking for new work, I had a phone call which was to change my life and my approach to Africa. The call was from Jim Mason, an old friend of mine from Serving in Mission (SIM) with whom I had done a lot of business over the years. He had started the Challenge Bookshops in Nigeria and Ghana. Jim asked if I was up for helping with a commentary written by Africans. I said "yes." In the same time period, I also said yes to a part-time job at Langham Literature (then called the Evangelical Literature Trust), and I also started my own company, Piquant Editions and Agency, indulging my interest in the arts and mission.

In 2000 Jim and I went on a "listening" journey through Africa to see if there was any vision for an African commentary. We found out that there were indeed African scholars with the same vision, which had arisen from the Pan African Leadership Assembly (PACLA) and the South African Christian Leadership Assembly (SACLA). We connected with Dr. Tokunboh Adeyemo and together we set about choosing a team of editors. Dr. Ngewa and Dr. Habtu, both from Nairobi Evangelical Graduate School of Theology (NEGST) (now Africa International University [AIU]) in Kenya, became the Anglophone New Testament and Old Testament editors, and Dr. Coulibaly and Dr. Andria, both from Faculté de Théologie Évangélique de l'Alliance Chrétienne (FATEAC) in Côte d'Ivoire, became the Francophone New Testament and Old Testament editors. Added to this team was a team of advisors, with Dr. Bediako and Dr. Turaki as our main consultants. They first set about brainstorming what it is to be "African," and what a "contextualized" commentary should look like. Next, they selected the contributors, Anglophone and Francophone, men and women. As Westerners we had no say in the selection of the contributors, nor in the theological content of the work.

But there was a challenge! Similar projects had been launched in the past, and they had all failed to materialize despite the investment of a lot of money and time. To make sure that this would not happen to the new project, we set down a number of publishing parameters: It should be a one-volume rather than a multivolume commentary. It had to be African. It had to be aimed at the pastoral market. The writers should have a PhD or be working towards one. In one or two cases, we allowed senior pastors with wisdom and experience to write. And lastly, it should be an evangelical commentary along the lines of the *New Bible Commentary*, and it should also include seventy-plus articles dealing with African realities. We also insisted that ownership of the commentary should remain in Africa. The Association of Evangelicals in Africa (AEA) became the owner of the project.

I felt that for the first time I was in true partnership. I was not "helping" but enabling, serving as a catalyst. And as I listened to the conversations and the decisions being made by my African brothers and sisters, it became very clear to me what was really needed: African theologians have much to say and to write, and we should make their voices heard.

The *Africa Bible Commentary* (*ABC*) project was sponsored by SIM, while Langham helped with the logistics. At first, many were skeptical about the project, but when Zondervan (with the visionary support of Dr. Stan Gundry) signed up to publish the commentary outside Africa, perspectives changed overnight. We also found a local publisher, WordAlive in Nairobi, and so three years before publication, everything was in place.

One of the realities we faced was the lack of good African editors who could handle such a large project. In the end, we had to choose an editor from the West, but one with plenty of cross-cultural and African experience. She was well accepted by the scholars, but she was a second choice. We need to come alongside to raise up good African editors for the African publishing enterprise, for without them Africans will struggle to find their own voice.

In 2006 the *ABC* was launched in Nairobi by Daniel Arap Moi, the former president of Kenya. At the launch, it became clear to me and everyone present that this project was truly Africa's! Looking around at my African colleagues, I realized how much they had taught me in these years about true partnership and how much *I* had needed "help."

A year later the *ABC* was published in French to great acclaim in Côte d'Ivoire. Since then, it has been published in Swahili, Malagasy, Portuguese, Hausa, and Amharic. It has also inspired other regional, contextual commentaries around the world—to date in South Asia, the Middle East and North Africa, South America, and the Slavic region.

From the beginning, we were hoping that the *ABC* would provide a springboard for other contextual and theological books written by Africans. A collection of publishers (ACTS in Nigeria, WordAlive in Kenya and Langham) came together to start Hippo Books. We asked the *ABC* board to be our advisors and away we went. I was excited, too excited as it turned out, and after five years I found I was largely the driving force keeping it moving. On realizing this, I handed over full editorial control to the *ABC* board, who now make all the final decisions.

The main reason for Langham getting involved with African publishing was the lack of academic publishers in Africa. In Kenya there were Acton and WordAlive (which no longer publishes academic books), and for the Catholic market there was Pauline Publications. In South Africa, there is Cluster in Pietermaritzburg, and in Malawi there is Kachere, but most other African publishers (and there are only a few) focus on more popular books. And all of these African publishers face major logistic hurdles when it comes to distributing their books across Africa.

It clearly was not enough for us just to encourage African academics to write. They were already writing. Again and again when discussing books with African theologians I heard about manuscripts that had been lying on someone's desk for one or two years and nothing seemed to be happening. Or academic works were being self-published without proper editing and with limited distribution. Furthermore, I was constantly asked whether we could publish PhD dissertations so that the fruit of their research would be more widely available. The African scholars had found that there were no publishers for dissertations in Africa, and that if they published their dissertations in the West, they were priced too high for any library in Africa.

In the end, I could see no other option than to start Langham Publishing, which gives a voice to authors not just in Africa but across the Majority World (MW). Not only could we publish their work in an affordable way but we could also make their books widely available, ensuring that Majority World theologians would be read in the rest of the world. So at last there is a constant stream not from the West to the MW, but rather from the MW to the MW and from the MW to the West. Our experience has, however, made it clear to us that a MW academic publisher needs to be global if it is to be able to sustain itself, and that it also needs additional grant income. Purely local academic publishing is unsustainable in MW countries because of the shortage of qualified personnel, the problems in raising capital, and the size of local markets.

Many African academics have been published in the last few years, and the younger generation of theologians are keen to publish African textbooks and African monographs in English and French through the likes of Hippo Books, which works closely with local publishers whenever possible. So African Christian Textbooks (ACTS) in Nigeria, Editions Clé in Cameroon, Les Presses Bibliques Africaines (PBA) in Benin, and Centre de Publications Évangéliques (CPE) in Côte d'Ivoire all partner to make this African dream come true. Langham Publishing also works closely with other MW publishing houses around the world, especially in providing books in various major languages.

There is currently another academic publishing initiative being undertaken in Kenya and Uganda with the help of SPCK Worldwide. It is known as the Africa Theological Network Press and is run by Kyama Mugambi, of the Centre for World Christianity at the Africa International University, Nairobi. We need to pray for this and similar initiatives.

Publishers everywhere are struggling because large bookshops have closed their doors, unable to withstand the pressure from technological giants. Certain Western authors are marketed as superstars while the rest struggle to survive, with many resorting to self-publishing unedited manuscripts. This applies to all types of publishing, including academic publishing, and it also applies in Africa. But in Africa there is the additional challenge of changing the engrained marketing slogan "the West is best" and replacing it with "Africa's writers for today."

There is much that Africans can learn from African theologians. I look forward to the day when African students have a plethora of homegrown textbooks and libraries filled with the academic fruit of Africa's greatest minds, edited by African editors. At present, too many African books are still being written and edited from a Western perspective. There is a pressing need for African books that address theology in a contextual manner and so deal with African issues and questions. When such books become available, African students and scholars will recognize themselves in what they read and become who they are, and who they are called to be.

I am convinced that the more contextual African theologians are, the more useful their books will also be for those of us outside Africa. As we see how African theologians move from the biblical text to the questions being asked in their communities, we will learn from their approach and their ideas, and gain insights into our own theology and our own communities.

PETER CALVIN

Christian Publishing
in a Majority Muslim Country

LIVING IN A PREDOMINANTLY Muslim country like Pakistan poses some unique challenges for the Christian minority. According to a conservative estimate, 1.5 percent of Pakistan's population of 220 million is Christian.[1] This means there are more than three million people in Pakistan who claim Christianity as their religion. The Christian community has managed to continue to exist and, to some extent, thrive in a country that has a growing tendency of hostility towards minorities, including Christians. The Christian Publishing House (MIK) is located in the heart of Pakistan, in Lahore, and has been publishing Christian books for the last seven decades.[2] MIK's ministry has gone through a progressive growth in these years. But the last four decades have caused MIK to face a growing adverse situation, which has eventually brought some dramatic changes in the publishing ministry.

THE CHRISTIAN PUBLISHING HOUSE (MIK), 1948–1980

The birth of the Christian Publishing House (MIK) can hardly be separated from the birth of Pakistan. The idea of MIK came into being when the majority religious groups—Hindus and Muslims—were demanding separate homelands from British rule in India. Their struggle resulted in the birth of

1. Pakistan Bureau, "Population by Religion."

2. MIK is an abbreviation for Masihi Ishaat Khana, which is the Urdu translation of "Christian Publishing House."

18

India (with Hindu majority areas) and East and West Pakistan (with Muslim majority areas). Yet, at that time, the subcontinent also hosted another religious community—the Christians—many of whom would end up in the land today known as Pakistan. Facing the challenges of their survival in this newly established, predominantly Muslim state, they had many basic questions about their own existence: Who are we and why are we different? How can we continue to exist and thrive while sharing our faith with other religious groups?[3] It was during this time that a Canadian missionary named Dennis E. Clarke serving in India came to the conclusion that the best way to help this relatively small community was to publish Christian books. Thus, the foundation of MIK was laid in 1948. The mission of MIK was, and remains today, to publish Christian books that strengthen Christians in their own faith, whilst enabling them to share their faith with the people of other religions living around them. And as Pakistan grew, so too did the Christian publishing work of MIK.

The Governance and Staff

Not only was MIK founded by a missionary, there was also strong missionary involvement both on the governance and administration level at MIK for the first three decades after its founding.[4] The board of trustees at that time and a sizeable number of the key staff were Western missionaries. Despite the earnest desire of the missionaries to let the local Christians manage and run MIK, it was not practically possible, as they still lacked good quality education and the training that such a task required.

The Published Books

Since the literacy level in the country was comparatively low, and even lower in the Christian community, most of the books published in the early years would trace their origins to Western culture. And although great efforts were made by Western missionaries to educate the Christian minorities of Pakistan, their efforts did not produce fruit in the form of a Christian community that was able to write books for their own local needs. Therefore,

3. See O'Brien, *Construction of Pakistani Christian*.

4. Information about the start and early years of MIK is available in the minutes book of the MIK board of trustee meetings, which is securely placed at MIK, 36 Ferozepur Road, Lahore.

most of the publications of MIK in those early years were translations of books originally written and published in the West. These books, despite all their strengths, failed to fully meet the felt needs of the local readers. MIK did all that could be done to adapt these Western books to meet the needs of Eastern society—for example by changing Western names to local ones and replacing Western illustrations with ones more appropriate to the Pakistani context—but somewhere, somehow, they were not able to fully serve the purpose. At the same time, these books were often perceived by non-Christians as a Western product and as such, labeled as Western propaganda. Eventually many came to see Christianity as a Western religion.

Religious Freedom

Pakistan, until 1980, could well be described as a moderate Islamic state. Christians did not face the threat of being persecuted for saying or writing anything that aimed to present the Christian message. In other words, there was enough freedom to practice and share the Christian faith without much fear. This comparatively free religious climate during the first thirty years enabled MIK to present the Christian message through various categories of books. Evangelistic books could even comprise comparative studies (apologetics) of Christianity with other religions. Biographies of people who were converted to Christianity could be published without being questioned or without resulting in persecution.

Furthermore, despite the limited resources, the distribution of these books was not a major obstacle. Anyone could visit one of the few Christian bookstores and buy the books of their choice without any fear of being labeled as someone trying to drift away from Islam and move to another religion. Many individuals, passionate to share the Christian message, would carry books in a shoulder bag and sell them without any fear of being trapped into saying something that could be considered to be, or fabricated as, blasphemy. Mobile book vans enjoyed great freedom in distributing MIK books. Then came a new wave of Islamic rules and regulations that gradually changed the whole scenario of Christian publishing.

THE CHRISTIAN PUBLISHING HOUSE (MIK), 1980–PRESENT

At the end of 1979 when the war between Russia and neighboring Afghanistan broke out, Pakistan felt she could not remain a silent spectator. General Zia ul Haq, the military leader who later became the president of Pakistan, believed that introducing more Islamic rules in the country was one of the best ways to prepare both the military and the whole nation against any more Russian expansion beyond Afghanistan. Therefore he started a strong wave of Islamization in the 1980s.[5] The increased prominence of Islamic beliefs upon Pakistani legal and social life has had important ramifications for Christian publishing. The most direct impact has come through the introduction of a series of blasphemy laws. These laws in themselves do not carry any harm as the aim is to protect the respect of every religion. However, problems have come through its misuse. Another impact that became stronger with the passage of time was on Western involvement. Missionary visas for any mission work, including MIK, became harder to get; translated books came to be considered Western propaganda.

Since there were quite a few different religious groups living in the Indian subcontinent at the time of colonization, the British government introduced laws in 1860 to protect the rights of these religious groups. These laws were further modified in 1927. So in a way, Pakistan inherited laws aimed at protecting and giving respect to the many religions being practiced in this large country.[6] Then, between 1980 and 1986, clauses were added to these existing laws. The present blasphemy laws could be summarized as: the use of derogatory remarks spoken, written directly or indirectly, or willful and malicious acts through words and actions, aimed to insult the holy Quran or the holy Prophet (PBUH). Violation of such laws carries a potential death sentence. Although the blasphemy law was meant to prevent religious violence, in fact it has been used to target vulnerable groups like Christian, Ahmadiyya Muslim, and Hindu minorities.

With the new laws relating to blasphemy imposed in the country, Christian publications have gone through a dramatic change. Experience has shown us that anything, and especially the written word, can be interpreted very differently by Christians and Muslims, and this has sometimes led to blasphemy charges. As a result, MIK does not take any chances when

5. Hussain, "What Went Wrong."
6. BBC, "Blasphemy Laws."

it comes to this highly volatile issue. Indeed, there have been many cases in the country where fake charges of blasphemy were fabricated against Christians. This often happens when a Muslim gets angry with a Christian and resolves to settle personal grudges by bringing the blasphemy charges against him or her. Asia Bibi is a prime example of such a scenario. She was accused of blasphemy in a village in Punjab in 2009. In 2010 she was sentenced to death. But in 2019 after a long ordeal of nine years in prison, the supreme court of Pakistan overturned the previous verdict because of lack of concrete evidence. According to various human rights groups, more than 1,500 cases of blasphemy were registered in various parts of Pakistan. About 75 percent of the accused were killed even before reaching a court decision. Of those who were killed, thirty-nine were Muslim, twenty-three Christian, nine Ahmadi, two Hindu, and two unknown.[7] Once you are charged with blasphemy it is unlikely that you will be found not guilty of it, because very few would testify against those who brought charges against Christians. Even the judges deciding such cases are under tremendous pressure to arrive at a decision against the accused. MIK fully realizes the potential misuse of this law; so the following measures have to be taken when choosing and preparing books for publication.

In the first place, MIK makes a policy of not mentioning Islam and especially their Prophet. Religion is embedded in almost all the areas of life in Pakistan. Almost all the Muslim homes in Pakistan organize some kind of religious teaching for their children from an early age. So Islamic teaching becomes a part of their life, just as it does for many Christians. The doctrines about God, the sinfulness of man, forgiveness of sins by God, the prophets and their role in bringing God's message to the human race, the temporality of life on earth, and eternal life hereafter are the key teachings given to each Muslim. Many of these teachings are, in one way or the other, contradictory to what the Bible teaches. In order to make an effective presentation of the Christian message to a Muslim living in Pakistan, it is very important that both Islamic and Christian teachings are presented parallel with full honesty and that the reader is allowed to choose that which appeals to his/her heart. This used to be an acceptable way of presenting the Christian message through comparative studies. However, this has not been possible since the early 1980s as such comparisons may be seen to be putting down Islamic teachings and proving Christian teachings to be superior. This has certainly reduced the scope of good and effective evangelistic writings but

7. Tarar, "In Pakistan."

has not eliminated the possibilities of presenting the Christian message to the Islamic world of Pakistan. MIK is now increasingly using the Common Ground Principle.

Indeed, while there are critical differences between the theologies of Islam and Christianity, there are a number of subjects and personalities that are common to both. MIK is using these commonalities to build understanding and relationships with Muslims, who may then come to see the theological differences between the two religions for themselves. For example, in both Islam and Christianity, there are patriarchs—Abraham, Jacob, Joseph—and prophets like Moses, David, and Elijah that are shared and where one can find a number of similarities in both religions. Therefore, the Christian message can be presented by talking about these. But what would MIK do when differences about key matters come into play? For example, the account of Abraham offering his son as a sacrifice to God is a major point of difference. Here, according to the policy of presenting biblical teaching only, MIK would simply lay out the sacrifice of Isaac as stated in the Bible and not mention what Islam says about this, or why. One big problem in this non-comparative approach is that it can leave the reader, who has learned these things from Islamic teaching, in a quandary and does not lead him/her to refute one idea and accept the other. So, the reader may have follow-up questions that would need to be answered. These questions could have been avoided if MIK was putting parallel teaching on the same subject and setting forth reasons why biblical teaching on that subject should be accepted. This was certainly not such a big issue for publishing in Pakistan prior to 1980. So, in a way, one can say that in post-1980 Pakistan, Christian publishing is being handicapped due to strict Islamic laws.

The Impact of Islamization

A second area of note is the need for indigenous writers. As mentioned above, most of the books published until the 1980s were translated from English to Urdu, and there were two main issues related to the publication of translated books, which are still relevant. Firstly, the non-Christian readers often understand these books as coming from a Western religion, and secondly, the Western books do not fully meet the felt needs of local readers. At the same time, the problem was that the Pakistani Christian community did not have trained writers. By the end of the 1980s MIK realized that we needed to publish books that were written by local writers.

23

By then there were more educated Christians than there had been three decades ago. However, very few Christians were willing to write, because the education system did not promote and encourage creative writing, and even if someone was remotely interested, there was not enough hope of bettering one's life by writing books. This has meant that MIK has had to go out of its boundaries in Christian publishing and start attracting and training educated and gifted people to write for local needs. To achieve this, in the early 1990s MIK began Writers' Workshops at least twice a year. This has continued even until now. These three- to five-day workshops are primarily arranged in Lahore. They consist of a combination of lectures (teaching) and written exercises (practical). The participants of these workshops are mostly young people, both men and women. Since stories are still one of the most popular genres in Pakistan, MIK initially gave more time and energy to train participants of the workshops in story writing. We thank God that, after the hard labor of these workshops, MIK is now self-sufficient in publishing stories written by local writers and has now started training writers in the area of article writing. The writings of the workshop participants are published in a digest "Kirnen" (Rays of Light), which has greatly encouraged the new writers. Needless to say, the writings of local writers are proving more effective as they address the very needs of local readers. In one of the workshops, one writer produced an excellent horror story with a meaningful Christian message. There are also stories on the subjects of love marriage or arranged marriage (a topic of special interest in Pakistan), interfaith marriages and their consequences, the curse of debt among the poor community, and abuse of Christian ministries by pastors and CEOs of Christian organizations. These are good stories and are making a great impact on local readers.

Another impact that Islamization has had is that fewer and fewer Western missionaries receive permission to work in Pakistan. This affects our publishing work in a number of ways. MIK must find godly, trained and gifted local Christians to serve on the board of trustees and others to work as staff members. The missionaries of the 1980s helped prepare us for this problem quite effectively by employing and training several young men with university degrees for the editorial department, which is the backbone of MIK's ministry. Of those who were employed in the early '90s, two have now been serving for more than twenty-five years and have been commended for their contribution to MIK's ministry. I am privileged to be one of the two. I joined MIK in October 1990. The present board of trustees is also comprised of Pakistanis. They come from various Christian ministries and have been faithfully carrying out the governance of MIK.

MIK finances faced a very different situation as the missionaries left the country and local Christians joined the staff. MIK needed more money to pay salaries of a bigger number of local staff, while some overseas funds that had been associated with the missionaries working in Pakistan were now not available to MIK. On the other hand, MIK has never been able to generate lots of revenue locally from the sales of its books, the reason being that Christian books are not among the first priorities of people when it comes to investing for their life. Therefore, in order to encourage people to buy books, MIK needs to make them available at an affordable price, which actually incurs financial loss and consequently increases dependency on donations.

It is an established fact that donors are not interested in ministries that need perpetual donations. So MIK has faced a much deeper problem in financial matters in these last forty years. Thanks to good policies of the board and effective training in the field of marketing and sales, there have been some concrete efforts from the administration of MIK to come out of dependency on donations. The last three decades have seen a gradual shift in the right direction.

During the last four decades MIK has seen a strong Islamic influence in every area of life. This has greatly impacted MIK's ministry in publication, personnel, and finances. As we look back on the past it is easy to see some positive and some negative things about the first thirty years of MIK's life, and the same is true for the last forty years, but overall MIK's ministry has grown considerably. The general reaction of the readers of MIK books suggests that in the last four decades MIK has published books that are more relevant to the local needs. MIK is governed and run by local Pakistanis and financially MIK is moving towards a better position of sustainability.

BIBLIOGRAPHY

Hussain, Touqir. "What Went Wrong: The Islamization of Pakistan 1979–2009." https://www.mei.edu/sites/default/files/publications/2009.07.Islamization%20of%20Pakistan.pdf.

O'Brien, John. *The Construction of Pakistani Christian Identity*. Pakistan: Research Society of Pakistan, 2006.

Pakistan Bureau of Statistics. "Population by Religion." http://www.pbs.gov.pk/content/ population-religion.

Tarar, Mehr. "In Pakistan, the Merciless Assassin: The Blasphemy Law." *Gulf News*, November 29, 2019. https://gulfnews.com/world/asia/pakistan/in-pakistan-the-merciless-assassin-the-blasphemy-law-1.1574945068960.

"What are Pakistan's Blasphemy Laws?" BBC News, May 8, 2019. https://www.bbc.com/ news/world-asia-48204815.

WONSUK MA

Publishing as Christian Hospitality: Experiences in Baguio and Oxford

I AM A KOREAN Pentecostal who stumbled into Christian publishing in the Philippines and went on to work in publishing in England. From my child-hood, I was always fascinated by the fresh ink smell of a new book. The sensation experienced by holding a new book shaped my childhood desire to become a bookstore keeper. I grew up in an era when every family tried hard to survive in post-war South Korea, and learning was reserved only for children as the grown-ups put everything they had into keeping the family afloat. As I grew up, I knew part of my dream would have to do with books. This hunch may, in part, have come from the long-standing high view of learning in East Asia.

This essay is a self-reflection of my journey as an editor, first in Asia and then in Oxford. My time in the Philippines was spent on Asian and Pentecostal subjects, while in Oxford, I focused on global and holistic mis-sion studies. In both cases, my role was to bring the voice of the churches of the southern continents (or global South) to the West-dominant global publishing market. The timing couldn't have been better: a radical shift was taking place in global Christianity, and advancing technologies had been revolutionizing the publishing industry. As each segment is presented here, I will discuss the challenges and new developments I experienced.

BAGUIO: UNDERSTANDING REGIONAL CHRISTIAN PUBLISHING

I served at Asia Pacific Theological Seminary (APTS) in Baguio City, Philippines as a missionary instructor (1983–2006). In this Pentecostal institution, both students and faculty members hardly had any materials published by Asians or on Asian Pentecostalism. During my student days, we Asians bemoaned the lack of Asian materials, especially given the age-long emphasis upon learning in our culture. Without knowing what was involved in the production and dissemination of such new knowledge, some of us began to dream of publishing Asian-authored materials for the Asian church. Two young American minds also joined our dream. Thus, the first Asian Pentecostal periodical was born in 1985: *Horizon: A Communication Paper of the Far East Advanced School of Theology*. Unfortunately, this inaugural issue was the first and last one that appeared! Although I had the delight of seeing my first published article, we all quickly learned that passion alone wouldn't make Christian publishing happen. Yet, my passion for Asian publishing on Pentecostalism steadily grew.

The next opportunity came ten years later when I decided to produce a volume of essays to honor an esteemed Pentecostal scholar, William Menzies, who served as president of the seminary. My good friend and the honoree's son Robert Menzies, who was with me in the failed journal attempt, joined me as my co-editor. Conscious of the possibility of creating a new intellectual space, we agreed to equally divide the list of contributors between the West and Asia. Almost all the Asian authors published their first studies in this book, *Pentecostalism in Context: Essays in Honor of William W. Menzies* (1997). However, the question of who would publish this book was a serious one. Ideally, we wanted an Asian publisher with a good reputation and a worldwide distribution chain, but there was none available to us. We did this before the era of print-on-demand (POD) technology and online marketers, such as Amazon.com. We had to rely on a Western publisher who was hospitable to this project, one with unknown authors whose names were difficult to pronounce and with questionable marketing potential. We found a wonderful friend in the *Journal of Pentecostal Theology* supplement series of Sheffield Academic Press (UK). After *Pentecostalism in Context* was published, our team went on to produce a similar project with the same publisher, which likewise featured emerging

Asian Pentecostal scholars.[1] Through these experiences, I became aware of the fact that new Asian scholars had much to share but that only Western publishers had the resources to produce their books and internationally market them.

Our search for a global (that is, Western at that time) publisher might be justified as both titles we produced were "global" in scope and subject matter. However, when I planned two subsequent edited titles on Asian subjects, I decided to use local publishers. A conference I organized in Manila became another volume.[2] It was my delight to discover and publish with a fine Christian publisher in the country with a reasonable marketing network in Asia. By the time two other colleagues and I organized an academic volume on David Yonggi Cho, the founder and (then) senior pastor of the world's largest Yoido Full Gospel Church,[3] APTS Press of Asia Pacific Theological Seminary was in operation. Although only indirectly involved in the establishment of this ground-breaking publisher, I wholeheartedly supported its program, which was a rarity among a dozen or so graduate theological institutions in the Philippines.

Another important initiative I undertook was journal publishing. The launch of the *Asian Journal of Pentecostal Studies* (1998) was a natural expression of two developments. The first was the serious commitment of APTS to serve as a hub for studies in Asian Pentecostalism. Several unique courses were added on the subject for various degree programs, while post-graduate programs were in development, such as Master of Theology and later Doctor of Philosophy (in cooperation with University of Wales). The second was the organization of the Asian Theological Society in Seoul (1998) as the world's Pentecostal leaders came together for a triannual celebration of the Pentecostal World Fellowship. Present were Dr. William Menzies and Dr. Vinson Synan, two of the three founders of the Society for Pentecostal Studies, and many emerging Asian thinkers such as Rev. Lim Yeu Chuen of Malaysia. This semiannual journal has become a fresh new space for sharing new studies and engaging with other church traditions. The journal has played an important role in strengthening the seminary's reputation as the research hub for Asian Pentecostalism. In the following year, the *Journal of Asian Mission* followed and published mission research in Asia, which I gifted to the Asia Graduate School of Theology,

1. Ma and Menzies, eds., *Spirit and Spirituality*.
2. Ma and Ma, eds., *Asian Church and God's Mission*.
3. Ma, Menzies, and Bae, eds., *David Yonggi Cho*.

an evangelical consortium of Asia Theological Association offering post-graduate programs. Although the editorial work of the journals took me many nights to learn desktop publishing, secure Asian scholarship, and find money for printing, I experienced a rare delight in seeing many fellow Asians publish their studies, often for the first time in the journals.

OXFORD'S REGNUM BRINGING THE SOUTH TO THE CENTER

The next phase of my life was in a radically different setting: Oxford. And the institution I came to lead was equally different. The Oxford Centre for Mission Studies (OCMS) was known as a unique church and mission leadership training center, especially for the global South. Born out of the "radical evangelical" movement, which first made its presence known at the Lausanne Congress on World Evangelization (1974),[4] the school had steadily established an emerging discipline of "holistic mission" through its research and postgraduate programs.[5] Along with its PhD program, what is relevant to the present discussion is its publishing arm, Regnum Books International, and the quarterly journal, *Transformation*. Under the able leadership of Christopher Sugden, the first Regnum title appeared in 1992. By 2006, when I assumed leadership of the institution and the publishing operation, there were more than thirty-two titles on diverse topics, and the majority of the authors were from the Two-Thirds World (per the community's preferred language). My predecessors had established the Centre's reputation for robust evangelical engagement with social issues and preference of the global South. Regnum Books International also established regional operations: Regnum Africa, Regnum Asia, and Regnum USA. The genius of its operation was an active partnership with established Western Christian publishers, of which Paternoster's role was especially important.

My ambition to publish half a dozen titles per year was immediately met by an operational challenge at Paternoster. "Slipping one or two titles in the production line" had been the modus operandi, according to Jeremy Muddit of Paternoster. Six projects cannot be "slipped in" without noticing, he argued. Perhaps Regnum had outgrown its nest, I mused. In my limited

---

4. Tizon, *Transformation after Lausanne.*

5. Embracing the social dimension of human life as an evangelical mission agenda, this movement is known as "integral mission." For various aspects of holistic mission, see Woolnough and Ma, eds., *Holistic Mission.*

knowledge with technological advancement, I suspected that we could run this in house. That meant Regnum would undertake the editorial and production management along with marketing and promotion. I just needed a daring partner, and I found one: Tony Gray of Words by Design (Oxford). In addition to providing expert editorial help, Gray also helped Regnum market its books.

Two observations motivated this expansion plan: first, the center of global Christianity had moved to the global South, and secondly, OCMS was producing more PhD dissertations on holistic mission. With increasing confidence as an evangelical team, we saw the potential for Regnum to serve a broad constituency. Thus, we added a Studies in Global Christianity series to the existing Regnum Studies in Mission. The World Council of Churches (WCC), the Global Christian Forum, and the 2010 Edinburgh Missionary Conference 2010 became our new clients.

Concerning the latter, shortly before my arrival, the Church of Scotland initiated the Towards 2010 process to plan a centenary celebration of the landmark 1910 Edinburgh Missionary Conference. Given the "radical" identity of evangelical Christianity and our mission to serve the global church, OCMS became an important participant. Regnum made the audacious decision to publish all the studies of the Conference, not imagining that the Regnum Edinburgh Centenary Series would end up with thirty-five titles and two compendium volumes! For a small institutional press, as one commented, "[Regnum] delivered a punch far above its weight." With a four-person editorial committee headed by Knud Jorgensen and a modest fund allocated by the General Council of Edinburgh 2010 (good for seven to eight titles), the project began without knowing where and how it would end. For the conference, two hardbound pre- and conference volumes were ready for every participant. The series in total contains three conference volumes, eight study commission titles, alongside regional, ecclesial, and thematic volumes. The uniqueness of the series is its geographical and ecclesial breadth: bringing missional voices, experiences, and issues from both global South and North, and from almost every Christian ecclesial family. All the volumes were published through the gracious financial assistance of many churches and mission agencies. In addition to twenty-four global mission libraries that received the full series as a gift, more than fifty libraries in the global South received the set at a deep discount. Moreover, the editorial committee decided to make the whole content available for free online, surrendering most proceeds from the series.[6] OCMS leadership took this step under the conviction that Christian mission was not a privilege only for the "haves," and that mission doesn't have to be expensive. The initial series was completed in 2016, and two compendium volumes appeared two years later. This heavy weight-lifting was no small feat for OCMS and Regnum. With the increasing output, Regnum published twenty-two titles per year at its height. The publisher is now established as a global "knowledge" outlet privileging the "younger" churches in the South to have a voice, bringing cutting-edge mission agenda to the mission community, and inviting diverse church traditions to engage and dialogue with one another. Our current goal is to narrow the gap between mission scholarship and frontline practices.

LOOKING BACK AND LOOKING FORWARD

The radical shift in global Christianity in the last quarter of the twentieth century coincided with technological developments that critically affected the publishing industry. I experienced these changes in two contexts: Asian and Pentecostal, and global and ecumenical.

My zeal for and faith in publishing has led me from the beginning as a constant learner. As an editor, I have had the opportunity to empower scholarly minds to bring their contributions to the public. I have enjoyed seeing emerging scholars excited about their very first published article or chapter. Some have since flourished as established scholars. In this sense, an editor is a midwife both to the book and to scholars.

This gift of editing also has enriched my life. If I can serve as an Asian or global Pentecostal leader, especially in international gatherings, it is because of the networks I have built, in part, through publishing. During the Oxford years, Regnum reached out to sister publishers who were committed to the new voices in the global South. I regularly met with leaders of Langham Literature and SPCK to explore ways that we could encourage publishing programs in the global South.

Over the decades, technological advancement has fundamentally affected the way books are published and shared. This change and the rise of Christianity in the South have encouraged many publishers in Africa, Asia, and Latin America, both stand-alone and institutional, to bring more books to the global market. Print-on-demand technologies and global

6. See www.ocms.ac.uk/regnum/edinburgh.

marketers such as Amazon.com allow more people to have a viable presence on the global scene. However, there is still a long way to go before Southern churches will be able to contribute to the global intellectual community in a manner befitting their growth rate and size. There are still many periodicals published by institutions on these continents (as well as in Eastern Europe and the Pacific islands), but most are never indexed by global indexing services. Their online presence is limited, and hence, their contributions are not known.[7] Global theological portals such as Globethics.net are valuable resource depositories where thousands of books and periodicals are available for free. Still, such services are not widely known, even though Globethics is sponsored by the World Council of Churches. Perhaps technology is not the solution, but God's people are. It will take the commitment of his church to improve the imbalance between the churches of the flowering, but resource-poor South and the resource-rich, yet struggling North.

If I may, I propose a modest intermediary step to bring the publishing initiatives of the South to the global market. I would love to see a global POD established with regional POD partners to serve regional and institutional publishers, particularly in the global South, acting as their agent for order-fulfillment, promotion, and sales-related management. Entities such as Global Forum of Theological Educators and Theological Book Network may consider such a vital service.

What am I doing now? I just began my fifteenth edited volume. Now my world is "global" and "Spirit-empowered Christianity," a nice outgrowth of the Baguio and Oxford experiences.

BIBLIOGRAPHY

Ma, Wonsuk, and Robert P. Menzies, eds. *Spirit and Spirituality: Essays in Honor of Russell Spittler*. Sheffield: Sheffield, 2003.

Ma, Wonsuk, and Julie C. Ma, eds. *Asian Church and God's Mission: Studies Presented in the International Symposium on Asian Mission in Manila, January 2002*. Manila: OMF, 2003.

Ma, Wonsuk, William W. Menzies, and Hyunseong Bae, eds. *David Yonggi Cho: A Close Look at His Theology and Ministry*. Baguio City, Philippines: APTS, 2004.

Tizon, Al. *Transformation after Lausanne: Radical Evangelical Mission in Global-Local Perspective*. Oxford: Regnum, 2008.

7. Several such regional or institutional journals are hosted at the Digital Showcase site of Oral Roberts University: digitalshowcase.oru.edu.

Woolnough, Brian E., and Wonsuk Ma, eds. *Holistic Mission: God's Plan for God's People.*
Regnum Edinburgh Centenary Series. Oxford: Regnum, 2010.

IAN DARKE

Spanish Language Evangelical Christian Publishing in Latin America

PERÚ IN THE 1980s was facing serious challenges. The whole country was politicized. The national universities insisted that all students took courses on dialectical materialism and Marxism. Walls of city buildings were covered with slogans from every left-wing political group imaginable, including the radical Maoist group Sendero Luminoso (Shining Path). Traditional political elites had done little to improve the lot of the abandoned communities, both in the mountains and in urban shanty towns. The situation was a breeding ground for radicalism. Something needed to be done: but what?

Senderistas did not entertain dialogue: people were either for the revolution or were slowing it down. Those in the second category—including priests, civil servants, and aid workers—were simply murdered. The military response was a brutal catch-all approach, which explains the title of one investigation at the time: *Between Two Fires*. Indigenous people in the mountains didn't know which was worse: to fall in to the hands of the terrorists or the military. As a consequence many fled the impoverished mountain regions to seek safety in the capital city of Lima. However the shanty towns (*pueblos jóvenes*) could offer little safety, and even less housing, water and work. At that time it was estimated that 40 percent of the population of Lima lived in poverty, with an additional 40 percent in extreme poverty: 80 percent in total.

Despite the poverty of many, books have always been important in Perú. Several of its writers are well known in translation, and one, Mario Vargas Llosa, nearly became president of the country in 1990. In political wall graffiti the leader of Sendero Luminoso, Abimael Guzmán, was always shown with a book under his arm. Printed literature was important in the battle for the heart of Perú.

After some years of work in the UK connected with the International Fellowship of Evangelical Students (IFES), my wife and I arrived in Lima in 1985 with an invitation to work with the IFES Christian student group there, AGEUP (Asociación de Grupos Evangélicos Universitarios del Perú). I also taught mathematics in the Universidad Nacional Mayor de San Marcos.

Two experiences from that time stand out in relation to the challenges faced in bringing print materials from one culture to another. On one occasion we were handing out Christian leaflets at the entrance to a national university, only to find that most were being thrown to the ground. When we ran out we couldn't get more of the originals, printed in China, so we produced a batch on an ancient duplicating machine using the cheapest possible grey "bulky" paper. To our surprise these "poor quality" leaflets, which had exactly the same text, were cordially accepted. Why? The answer was simple. The first were clearly foreign. The second group were clearly "Made in Perú."

On another occasion, at a church in a poorer part of the city, we were talking about family issues. We lent out a translated book from the US about family discipline. While the untranslated original had been found to be helpful and biblical among American evangelicals, the translation caused confusion. One section discussed what to do if the son of the family wants to take a girl out on a date, borrowing the second family car. The book offers wise advice. However readers in Lima understood that the boy wanted the car to take the girl out in order to rape her! In their context no family had one car, let alone a second, and the culture of dating was worlds apart.

With these experiences in mind, and convinced of the need for sensible Christian materials that were culturally appropriate, a group of Peruvian friends and I set up a publishing enterprise called Ediciones PUMA. (The puma, or mountain lion, is indigenous to Perú, though it is in danger of extinction. For both reasons a suitable name for a national publishing company!) None of us had experience in publishing, though we did bring skills in design, computing, academia, and accounting. Most importantly, we had a passion to produce materials that were biblical and relevant to the lives of Peruvians.

In the years that followed, as the enterprise grew and we had more contact with Christian bookstores, we discovered something of the topsy-turvy world of Spanish language publishing in which for non-Christian booksellers the USA was a minority market, in contrast to Christian publishing, dominated precisely by the USA. Why this was, and its implications, were matters that affected us deeply.

Book publishing in general was vigorous not only in Perú but all of Latin America. There were high levels of literacy, and books were valued. Even in its worst time of crisis a Peruvian publisher of books on *chess* continued to survive. The countries with the strongest publishing programs were Argentina, Colombia, and Mexico, along with Spain of course. Argentina was home to some of the largest bookstores anywhere, and the international book fairs of Bogotá, Buenos Aires, and Guadalajara ranked amongst the most important in the world. General, secular publishing was vigorous and connected across country borders, including to one relatively minor market . . . the USA.

Book production for the Christian market was very different. First of all there was, and is, a huge gulf between Catholic and evangelical (Protestant) publishing. For historic reasons the vast majority of evangelicals would not touch Catholic books. And on the whole, Catholic bookstores would not sell evangelical books. With some important exceptions, they were worlds apart. As to the structure and dynamic of Catholic publishing, my impression is that it was similar to the wider world of *general* publishing in Spanish, in other words, with strong roots in Spanish-speaking countries. There were a number of highly regarded and long-standing Catholic publishers in Spain, and a publisher such as the Editorial San Pablo, a mission of the Society of Saint Paul, operated across Latin America.

However, *evangelical* publishing in Spanish was strangely different. It was based principally not in Latin America but in the USA, even though there was little general publishing in Spanish there. For distinct historical reasons there was also some evangelical Christian publishing in Spain. But from either source it was hard to find books with a distinctly Latin American flavor.

So, why was Spanish language Christian publishing based so much in the USA rather than in the continent where a far greater number of evangelicals live? When we looked back to the arrival of evangelicals in the late nineteenth and early twentieth centuries, it was clear that book distribution and other literature ministries played a significant role, despite difficulties due to opposition from Roman Catholic priests and others. In 1888 Francisco Penzotti arrived in the port of Callao, near Lima, on behalf of the Bible Society. Accused by a local priest of causing a disturbance by preaching heresy, he was taken prisoner, becoming something of a *cause celébre*. The case drew support from liberals shocked at religious intolerance. Positive attention was drawn to the work of the Bible Society, issues of freedom of religion, and to Bible reading. Before the turn of the century Christian bookstores and print houses, as well as evangelical magazine and book publishers were established across the continent.

The *Casa Bautista*, the Baptist publishing house, established in Toluca, Mexico in 1905, moved across the border to El Paso in 1917, due to political instability in Mexico. Other denominational publishing initiatives faced the economic roller coasters of Latin American republics for many years, until, with easier communication and travel, some said "why not move to Miami?"

A factor affecting publishers from the 1960s was the changed religious panorama of Latin America, and, along with it, the policies of missions and denominations. Books such as David Stoll's *Is Latin America turning Protestant?* (University of California Press, 1991) and David Martin's *Tongues of Fire* (John Wiley & Sons, 1993) documented the growth and the impact of evangelicalism in the continent during the second part of the twentieth century. With news of the growth of megachurches from Argentina to Mexico, and the profile of Latin American evangelists like Luis Palau serving the English-speaking world, some denominations and mission boards decided to shift policy, arguing that Latin America is "evangelized" and withdrew direct support to national agencies.

While the growth of evangelical churches has been truly transformative, what was not always considered seriously was the phenomenon of "nominal Christianity." Since the Spanish *conquista* of the continent, when Christian faith was imposed by the sword, the Roman Catholic church in Latin America has struggled with those who label themselves as Christian, but whose faith makes no impact on their lives. Now, could it be that people were merely switching from one label to another, from "Catholic" to "evangelical"?

Over the following years several of the mission or denominational based organizations, while seeking to continue to serve the church in Latin America, took a step further and decided to sell their USA-based Spanish language publishing operations. For example, Editorial Vida was created in the 1950s in Mexico as Pedro Press, as an organization of the Assemblies of God. It moved to Miami in the 1960s. In 1995 Editorial Vida was sold to the Zondervan Publishing Company. Subsequently Zondervan—including the Vida imprint—became part of the HarperCollins Group, owned by Australian-born media magnate Rupert Murdoch.

A second example is the Caribe Publishing House, which was formed by the Latin America Mission (LAM) in the 1940s. In 1968 Caribe became autonomous from Latin America Mission and then moved to Miami in 1969. During the 1980s economic problems affected the operation and by the 1990s Caribe was to form part of the Thomas Nelson publishing company, along with Editorial Betania from 1992. The original Thomas Nelson company—founded in 1798— had been taken over by the Thomson Organization in 1960. After further difficulties Thomas Nelson was subsequently bought from Thomson in 1969 by the National Book Company. Thomas Nelson is now, like Vida, a division of the HarperCollins Group.

Why would one of the world's largest general publishers like HarperCollins be interested in Spanish language Christian publishing? The answer perhaps lies in the growth of the Hispanic population in the USA. For companies based in USA it is far simpler to sell to the Hispanic community in the USA, so avoiding shipping charges, international customs duty, and delays in payment of bills. Added to this is the phenomenon of the cultural shifts experienced by new arrivals in the USA. Facing the need to develop new social frameworks and a new identity, in addition to freeing themselves from social and religious controls of the past, many immigrants are open to considering "the new" in that "Protestant" country. Hence, when a Christian bestseller hits the Walmart shelves in the USA, many immigrants may be interested to read the same book as their Anglo neighbors, but in Spanish, even with a matching cover. The quality of translation may be of secondary concern, as translators and readers alike live in a majority English-speaking world.

We are not saying that good books are not being produced in the USA, but there is a strong pull to publish mostly "popular" titles, in translation. For a (profit-based) US-based company, it would make less commercial sense to produce a translation of a Bible commentary, for example. Not only would it be much more expensive to produce than a motivational book, it is highly probable that an educated Spanish-speaking pastor who works in the USA would be able to read *English* well enough not to need a translation!

The US Hispanic community has its own issues related to migration, racism, and identity and a flourishing world of theological reflection, seminary studies, and the publication of resources, both in Spanish and in English, focused on the experiences of Hispanic communities of the US. Interesting as they may be, they are by definition of limited relevance to pastors and leaders in the completely distinct, much larger, and complex world of Latin America, coping with the violence, chaos, and poverty of a shanty town, for example.

In 1996 during a summit meeting of major evangelical organizations working in Latin America, it was agreed to act together to strengthen the production of relevant Christian books in the continent. A network of evangelical Christian publishers was formed—called Letra Viva (Living Letter)—to identify the challenges being faced, and to work together to strengthen Christian writing and publishing activity within the continent.

A priority for all publishers was to improve channels of distribution. Consequently one of the first activities of Letra Viva was to participate jointly in the newly established EXPOLIT book fair, a key place for interactions between publishers and Christian booksellers. If distributors and bookstores are not aware of the excellent books being produced, they cannot sell them!

As well as the promotion and distribution of books, another challenge concerned logistics. Letra Viva created a joint international Dispatch and Distribution Centre in the year 2000, providing warehouse space and shipping facilities out of Miami. Strange as it may seem, it can be simpler and cheaper to send books from Colombia to Argentina, for example, if they pass though Miami on the way! Smaller publishers have had to learn a lot about international shipping, consolidation of orders, and customs regulations. By 2016 the Letra Viva centre was closed as parallel distribution services were available, serving publishers well.

Concern to produce more books that are relevant to Latin America, and hopefully by Latin Americans, has been shared by many groups, including Cook Communications Ministries, MAI (Media Associates International), and the Langham Partnership. All have provided significant help in developing Christian writers and supporting the growth of Christian publishing within the continent.

One sign of the continuing need for relevant and Biblical materials has been the development from 2007 till 2019 of the *Contemporary Bible Commentary* (*Comentario bíblico contemporáneo*) written entirely from within Latin America, by more than one hundred Latin American scholars. Already some of these men and women have gone on to write articles and books, all with a Latin flavor, to serve the church.

Evangelical statesman Samuel Escobar, from Perú, notes that there is a danger of implosion of the evangelical church in Latin America, as many folk have been disappointed by the promises of "health and wealth" or prosperity theology. At the same time it has been encouraging to receive reports of an increasing demand for books with more substance, including those from the Reformed tradition and a renewed interest in Bible study.

So what will the future hold?

As far as technology is concerned, interest in ebooks has not been strong in any sector of publishing in the continent. Ereaders are rarely seen, though smart phones are ubiquitous, so phone publishing could grow. Digital print could be a great help if there were providers in each country.

Distribution continues to be a major concern. There are probably fewer bookstores than in the past, not so much due to online sellers but a loss of focus. Some bookstores were so used to selling imported "lighter weight" books from the US that they lost a public looking for more substantial books. With a lack of professionalism, many stores closed. A higher percentage of books are now sold directly to churches, at conferences, and at book fairs.

There is a continuing need for resources that help the church to grow in depth, to engage with the Bible, and to act as changemakers in every community. Thankfully there are a growing number of able communicators within the continent who have the capacity to produce the books that the Christian public is looking for.

Groups like Sendero Luminoso, so active decades ago, may be less of a threat now, but are replaced by new threats, including economic inequality, and political and drug-related violence. Publishers continue to face these challenges and, with a little help from their friends, they will flourish. God willing, we shall see more books "Made in Latin America."

FR. GIUSEPPE COSTA

Second Lesson: The Publishing House to the Popes

THE PUBLISHING HOUSE INSPIRED and desired directly by the Popes merits special attention, especially in recent times with Popes who can activate cultural processes with an aspect of modern interactivity that almost begin to follow the trends of the day.

Vatican publishing has a long and rich history. Its roots trace back to the sixteenth century with Propaganda Fide's publishing of reports on missions in Asia and America and with the publishing of early editions of the Bible.

Let's not forget that Gutenberg's invention was first used for printing the Bible.

The Vatican Typography has almost always identified with Vatican publishing and has experienced much of the same history. It would take a long time to discuss this history, a task not meant for this small manual.

In her essay *Gli Editori del Papa Da Porta Pia ai Patti Lateranensi*, Maria Iolanda Palazzolo outlined the main events. In this essay, Palazzolo examines the history of Vatican publishing from before the end of the Vatican State (1870) to the 1930s.[1] It should be recalled that, for many years, the Vatican made use of French, German, and Italian distributors who guaranteed the distribution of manuals, documents, and essays. Pustet, Desclèe, and Herder were important players and had rich catalogues of works prominent in the Catholic world.

---

1. Palazzolo, *Gli Editori*.

"In the first twenty years of the twentieth century," Palazzolo writes, "it had already become clear to everyone—politicians, jurists, public opinion —that the Roman Church wanted to equip itself with a financially independent and technologically advanced publishing house that could handle the publication and distribution throughout the world of official acts of the ecclesiastical government and works considered key to its ministry."[2]

In 1926, another step was taken towards full editorial autonomy. In *Acta Apostolica Sedis*, in fact, we find this brief note:

> As per new provision, the administrations of the Vatican Polyglot Typography and of the Vatican Publishing House have been made separate and mutually autonomous. Thus, in order to avoid probable confusion and to achieve the easy and timely handling of correspondence, that which concerns exclusively typographical work should be addressed to the Vatican Typography while anything concerning the purchasing or commissioning of books should be addressed to the Vatican Publishing House.[3]

Since the pontificate of Pope Pius XI, the typography had been run by the Salesians, who put their experience into graphic art until the recent 2018 reform that brought this experience to an end. The negative economic situation played a decisive role in this, as in many other cases.

It shows the editorial pragmatism of an institution that has an important relationship with books but that never fully assumed the role of a strong publishing company.

The works published by the Roman Pontiffs, beginning with Pope Pacelli and his great speeches, were broadcast over radio rather than distributed in print version, and are numerous enough to justify a medium-sized publishing house in the Vatican. That is precisely what happened when it was realized how important it is to own copyrights and to have a catalogue that would not only bring those works together but relaunch them in the international media context. While the publication of papal documents has had and continues to have an impact on the importance of Vatican production as well as its balance sheet, there have been a few specific publications that raised the Vatican Publishing House to new heights, placing it alongside large publishers (authors, the market, production, price of printing, rights, packaging and marketing, book fairs, important meetings, events).

---

2. Palazzolo, *Gli Editori*, 141.

3. *Acta Apostolica Sedis* vol. 18, no. 1, 400.

The first book to make an author out of a Pope, which raised a series of questions, was *Love and Responsibility* by John Paul II. The regulation of rights to papal and Vatican works, sought primarily by Cardinal Angelo Sodano in his May 31, 2005 decree, and the wealth of teachings from Popes such as Benedict XVI allow for the growth of an international market for rights to be sold anywhere and to all publishers. This has caused a domino effect that has led, among other things, to the Vatican Publishing House becoming profitable and each year contributing to the Pope's charity. These profits vary but have been consistent for at least the last fifteen years with net earnings of over 10 million euros.

The money earned from the sale of rights to Pope Benedict's works made it possible to create the Joseph Ratzinger Vatican Foundation, which has over 7 million euros donated by the Pope for theological research and for financial aid for deserving students. Ratzinger's works undoubtedly had a decisive influence on the growth of Vatican publishing. Just consider *Opera Omnia* and the three volumes of *Jesus of Nazareth*. The large print runs make them worldwide publishing events where the incomparable celebrity of Joseph Ratzinger, coupled with graphic and marketing choices, exalt the Vatican Publishing House, which many had until then considered to be a sort of typographic appendage rather than a true publishing house.

Like the first volume, Joseph Ratzinger's *Jesus of Nazareth: Holy Week: From the Entrance into Jerusalem to the Resurrection* (2011), is a complex and fascinating book that puts the Pope's "privilege of position" to good use with the exceptional authority in his word. This is confirmed, first of all, by the sales numbers for both works: *Jesus of Nazareth: From the Baptism in the Jordan to the Transfiguration* (2007) became an instant bestseller and has been translated in twenty-three countries, while the second volume has sold over two million copies (fifty thousand copies sold on the release date alone). It was the Pope who decided that the second volume should be published by the Vatican Publishing House, while the first and third volumes were published by Rizzoli.

This was the highlight of the last century for Vatican publishing. An exchange of letters between the director of the Vatican Publishing House, Fr. Giuseppe Costa, and Pope Benedict determined that the volume would be published in the Vatican (Vatican Typography and Publishing). Subsequently, more curial and institutional, rather than editorial, criteria began to take priority.

The Vatican Publishing House's participation at the Frankfurt Buchmesse and the Turin International Book Fair, as well as its presence in London, Warsaw, Malta, Santo Domingo, and at book fairs held in Los Angeles, Baltimore, and Philadelphia (organized by American Catholic publishers in collaboration with the Conference of Bishops) brought Vatican publishing into contact with other professionally relevant organizations.

This interaction sparked sizable growth in terms of quality for both the organization and its production. A look at the Vatican Publishing House's 2016 catalogue reveals how it succeeds, as Maurizio Gronchi wrote in the September 1, 2016 issue of *L'Osservatore Romano*, "in offering daily updates on the life of the Church which from the symbolic center of the community extends continuously to parts of the world where the Pope's word is awaited and embraced with trust and joy."[4]

Unfortunately, this qualitative and quantitative development was not taken into account by the reformation currently taking place after the Motu Proprio "For the Establishment of the Secretariat for Communication" issued on June 27, 2015. The Vatican Publishing House was incorporated into the Secretariat for Communication, which was made a dicastery by papal rescript in June 2018. To date, apart from some adjustments to the administrative organization, there are no certainties from an editorial and commercial point of view. Moreover, the Vatican Publishing House lacks the freedom of choice and decisions on markets that is indispensable to any editorial work. We have already seen the effects of a non-exhaustive and untimely production of the magisterium on the annual balance sheets after over ten years of positive growth.

The Motu Proprio points out that "'The current context of communications, characterized by the presence and development of digital media, by the factors of convergence and interaction, demands both a rethinking of the Holy See's information system, and a commitment to reorganize it, while appreciating what has been developed historically within the framework of communications of the Apostolic See, certainly moves towards a unified integration and management."[5]

Moreover, with the advent of Pope Francis's papacy came the trend of allowing interviews with Pope Francis to be released by relevant non-Vatican publications. And while the many introductions prepared by the Pope for books of mixed religiosity may have given an economic advantage

4. Gronchi, "Io sono Guiseppe vostro fratello."
5. Francis, *Motu Proprio*, lines 1–4."

to publishers such as Mondadori and Rizzoli, they have limited the distribution of the magisterium and slowed the domino effect that was created more than a decade ago. In conclusion, the logic of the publishing market, as well as the religious publishing market, differs from that of institutional information systems and the technological convergence that require new and particular skills.

BIBLIOGRAPHY

Acta Apostolica Sedis vol. 18, no. 1 (1926). http://www.vatican.va/archive/aas/documents/AAS-18-1926-ocr.pdf.

Palazzolo, Maria Iolanda. *Gli Editori del Papa Da Porta Pia ai Patti Lateranensi*. Rome: Viella, 2016.

Gronchi, Maurizio. "Io sono Guiseppe vostro fratello." *L'Osservatore Romano*, September 1, 2016. https://www.osservatoreromano.va/it/news/2020-06/io-sono-giuseppe-vostro-fratello.html.

Francis, Pope. "Apostolic Letter Issued Motu Proprio: For the Establishment of the Secretariat for Communication." http://www.vatican.va/content/francesco/en/motu_proprio/documents/papa-francesco-motu-proprio_20150627_segreteria-comunicazione.html.

JOSEPH SINASAC

From the Great Depression to the Digital Age: A Canadian Catholic Publisher's Journey

INTRODUCTION

In 2020, Novalis Publishing turned eighty-five years old, a rather vener-able age for a publishing house in the digital era. Publishing books used to be called a "gentleman's game," inspiring images of boozy lunches, or coffee-fueled meetings in smoky, dingy offices with wood-paneled walls, tweed suits, and lots of arguing over subordinate clauses and the place of commas. Maybe publishing was never actually like that. It certainly isn't now.

Though people continue to read, traditional publishers are in survival mode. It's no secret that the way people read and consume the printed word has undergone a revolution, transforming most radically the economic model that underpins publishing. Ebooks, audiobooks, online reading of free material, the retail juggernaut that is Amazon and its imitators, the introduction of digital learning into the classroom—all have conspired to force publishers to adapt or die.

In this essay, we'll look at how one religious publisher—Novalis—in one country—Canada—has attempted to adapt to the flood of challenges imposed by technical, social, and economic changes in the last twenty years. How successful it has been is still an open question. The best evidence of its success is, perhaps, the fact that it is still here, still serving the people of God as it has since 1935.

CHRISTIAN BOOKSELLING IN CANADA

Let's start with a quick survey of the state of the Christian world in Canada. Given that Novalis is owned by a community of Roman Catholic priests, and its main work has been within the Catholic world, the focus here will obviously be heavily weighted toward this denomination. While Novalis does reach out to other mainstream Christian denominations, there is no doubt that the Catholic Church and its many organizations are the primary focus of Novalis's publishing efforts.

That said, in Canada, Catholicism is the single largest Christian denomination and, in fact, the largest religious group. Roughly 12.8 million Canadians identify themselves as Roman Catholic, according to Statistics Canada. This represents 39 percent of the Canadian population. But such a large number hides some significant signs of retreat.

In recent decades, weekly church attendance has declined dramatically, hovering below 20 percent in English Canada and less than 10 percent in French Canada. Those numbers haven't declined even more thanks to large numbers of immigrants from countries such as the Philippines, India, Vietnam, and Korea.

While large urban centers such as Toronto continue to build new churches, more rural parts of the country are experiencing church closures and the combining of parishes.

Participation by age also shows wide variations. Older generations—the baby boomers—continue to participate in large numbers while those below thirty-five are noticeable by their absence.

Even Catholic schools are experiencing student population declines, largely because of lower birth rates. Canada has large publicly funded Catholic school systems in the provinces of Ontario, Saskatchewan, and Alberta, and partially funded schools in other provinces such as Manitoba and British Columbia. At one time, this represented about 750,000 students and 50,000 educators. In the last ten years, these numbers have dropped slightly.

The fate of Christian bookstores has been even more devastating. Within the last ten years alone, the number of these stores has declined by about 50 percent, leaving roughly 200 today to serve the entire country. Many of these are small mom-and-pop operations, surviving thanks more to the sale of church supplies such as candles and vestments than to books. The challenge then for Novalis has been to find ways to display its books to potential readers, given the lack of brick-and-mortar stores where they would have been traditionally found.

With the decline in participation, churches and affiliate organizations are facing reduced budgets. The first thing to go in such circumstances is print resources. This trend has been accelerated by the rise of online catechetical resources available through nonprofit organizations, mostly based in the United States. Organizations such as Dynamic Catholic and Formed in Faith offer modern supermarkets for religious education resources in a variety of media, including video, audio, and text. Being nonprofit, they can offer low-cost resources that can be readily distributed to parishioners.

Amazon has also had a major impact on how consumers buy religious books. With its free delivery options and deeply discounted prices, it has become a major challenge to bookstores and even Novalis's own online shopping site. It has become common to hear of consumers finding a Novalis title in a bookstore and going to Amazon to buy it. Per book, this represents a difference of 50 percent in revenue from what Novalis would earn if the book had been purchased directly from its website or sales representative.

WHERE NOVALIS FITS IN

A defining feature of Novalis over its eight-plus decades has been its adaptability. Each era posed new challenges, some of growth, some of decline. Some were technological or social. All required flexibility, creativity, and a willingness to take risks.

This publishing house was born in 1935 out of a Catholic Action conference in Ottawa, the nation's capital. André Guay, a priest of the Oblate Missionaries of Immaculate Mary, was among a group of fellow Oblates teaching at the University of Ottawa, then an Oblate-run Catholic college. He was challenged at this conference to create a center that would nourish the growing appetite among Catholic laity for accessible and affordable resources to help them deepen their faith. Out of this came the Catholic Centre and its firstfruits were Sunday worship booklets, the precursors to *Living with Christ* and *Prions en Église*.

Over the decades, Novalis published in a variety of forms. It created a marriage preparation program titled Mosaic that was translated into sixteen languages and used in twenty-five countries by a variety of Christian denominations. It also produced audiocassettes, pamphlets, church bulletins, and a wide range of booklets and books.

The turbulent 1960s were particularly heady times for Catholic publishing in Canada. The Oblates who ran both the University of Ottawa and the Catholic Centre gave new meaning to both institutions when they renamed the college as Saint Paul University in 1965 and the Catholic Centre as Novalis in 1969. *Novalis* has Latin roots, meaning "newly ploughed field ready for sowing."

The Church in the 1960s and 1970s was still going through its honeymoon with the Second Vatican Council. Attendance was still vigorous and church organizations were flowering. But already, the signs of the decay to come were present. Ordinations for priesthood declined and men and women left vowed religious life in droves. In the 1980s the first revelations of the clergy sex abuse crisis were appearing. This would become the defining crisis of the Catholic Church to date, coloring almost every initiative and inflicting extreme damage on the credibility of the Church.

In 2008, the Oblates at Saint Paul University decided to retire from publishing. Subsequently, the trademark and ownership of all its titles was transferred to the Augustinian Fathers of the Assumption, a community of priests started in France in the nineteenth century, with membership in countries around the world, including Canada. The Assumptionists have traditionally been involved with publishing through an enterprise called Bayard Presse. In Canada, Bayard Canada now owns Novalis, along with some nonreligious publishing entities.

The fortunes of Novalis are intimately tied to that of the Church. It's largest periodical, a worship aid called *Living with Christ* in English and *Prions en Église* in French, has seen its circulation slowly but steadily decline over the decades. In the late 1970s, the weekly editions of its French edition printed 650,000 copies. Today it is just under 200,000. The English edition, from a high of just under 100,000, is now about 65,000. Novalis responded in part with the publication of an annual missal, containing all the Sunday liturgies for the year. It remains a mainstay of the publishing program, continuing to sell almost 270,000 copies a year, remaining remarkably resistant to decline, largely because of its convenient form and affordability for parishes.

THE RESPONSE TO CHANGING TIMES

The story of Novalis Publishing is a story of adapting to change. But rarely has the pace of change been so rapid, or the circumstances so daunting. To avoid being swallowed by Amazon or eclipsed by online foreign competitors such as Dynamic Catholic, Novalis Publishing has had to go back to its roots and exercise a laser beam-like focus on those it has served since its earliest days, Canadian Catholics and their institutions.

Inside Novalis, the team talks about "embracing the niche." This means accepting that the churches, schools, and affiliated organizations want a publisher that understands their needs and can respond with customized resources. This overall strategy has a number of components:

- creating new titles by partnering with the people and organizations that ultimately use Novalis resources;

- keeping in close communications with the customers in order to be intimately aware of their latest initiatives, or how they are being forced to change by circumstances;

- creating a community of "friends" around the Novalis brand through social media and events;

- increased sponsorship and attendance at events that support the Novalis community;

- marketing efforts that are multimedia and tailored to particular groups;

- strict refocusing of publishing efforts away from speculative titles to those with clear markets.

Each of these six strategies involves different members of our publishing team at different times and places. I will expand here on each.

The most important facet of any publishing house is its authors. As a pan-Canadian publishing house, operating in a near vacuum when it comes to domestic competition, Novalis has a responsibility to make room for authentic Canadian voices within the religious world. While many potential authors come knocking on the Novalis doors unsolicited, given its dominant position, this is not enough to ensure Novalis is finding the best writers and ideas available.

In English Canada, this means getting out of the office and finding out what people are talking about, where they are gathering. Some of this can be done through regular social media monitoring, checking blogs, websites, Instagram, etc. But there is no substitute for face-to-face interaction. In reality, the search must take place at all levels.

That means having senior editorial staff attending significant conferences across the country for teachers, pastoral assistants, clergy, vowed religious, catechists, chaplains, etc. Often an editor will accompany sales representatives to such events, with the editors attending workshops to listen to potential authors and meet with them to discuss potential writing projects. Here's what they are looking for: people with something interesting to say, who can say it well, and have already found an audience. Such authors often have a lively social media presence with an eager following. For them, having a book to add to their resume can build their credibility and offer another source of income.

One of the bestselling Novalis books of the last five years originated this way. The editor was attending a high school chaplains' conference near Toronto in 2012, at which he listened to a Fr. James Mallon discussing the New Evangelization of Pope Benedict XVI. A brief meeting with Fr. Mallon afterwards led to a two-year discussion about a potential writing project. The ultimate fruit of this was *Divine Renovation: From a Maintenance to a Missional Parish*, a 2014 book on parish renewal based on Fr. Mallon's own experiences in parish life and his reading of Scripture and papal teachings. This book touched a live chord in Catholic parishes around the world. Fr. Mallon was in great demand as a conference speaker and his "Divine Renovation" program became an apostolate, complete with multimedia tools, coaching teams, and international events. The original book has almost 100,000 copies in print, in about ten languages. For religious publishing, this is a true success story.

A second aspect of this activity is partnering with organizations that need customized resources. Religious communities, Catholic school districts, even dioceses are often looking for ways to economically publish books of history, prayers, or catechesis customized for their particular needs. Through creative negotiations, Novalis has been able to publish titles whose costs are covered by the organizations commissioning them. Typically, Novalis will print enough to meet the needs of the organization, plus a smaller number to sell more widely. Recently, Novalis has included roughly two such projects in each fiscal year.

One of the more interesting series along these lines was the Jesuit History project. In this three-volume series, Novalis published scholarly histories of the Jesuits' work in English Canada since the arrival of the first Jesuit priests. The authors were all Jesuit scholars and the series editor was well-known Canadian historian Jacques Monet, SJ. The Jesuits agreed to buy a certain number of copies of each issue, with the rest available for general distribution. In this way, an important part of the history of this country was preserved.

In support of the publishing efforts, Novalis has tried to build its presence within the Catholic community in a number of ways. In the last ten years, the number of conferences attended by editorial and sales representatives has tripled to about twenty a year—a significant number for a small publisher covering the vast geography that is Canada. At the same time, Novalis has increased its sponsorship budget to help ensure that such events continue. These have also been supplemented by select focus groups for discussing particular subjects or potential projects. These have ranged from groups of Catholic educators, young Catholics, or pastors. In this way, specific publishing projects have been refined to better meet the needs of their users. Such discussions have the added benefit of building a sense of community and ownership for Novalis books among those customers.

So far, the discussion has focused on traditional communication with customers. This has not precluded the use of e-commerce and online social media. Such tools are complementary to face-to-face contact. A Facebook page, a blog called Seeds of Faith, a monthly newsletter, weekly e-blasts to selected audiences—all help build awareness of Novalis and create a sense of community.

This shift in focus has meant a corresponding change in direction for the publishing program itself. From about forty-five titles a year, the English program has reduced output to about twenty-five new titles. Only about one-third of these are what would traditionally have been known as "trade" titles, that is, of interest to a broad public and widely available in secular bookstores. Increasingly, new titles are the results of collaborations with partners or finely tuned to the needs of the end readers. Or they are better classified as "resources," books used to support training or educational programs such as sacramental preparation for children, which are purchased annually.

Marketing, too, has had to shift to support the changing list. E-blasts focused on particular groups, such as Catholic teachers or pastors, are increasingly common. Book launches are tied to education or pastoral conferences to take advantage of the gathering of the optimum audience for a particular title. Finally, Novalis, which has long acted as a distributor of books from non-Canadian religious publishers, has positioned these efforts as a "one-stop shopping" experience for those requiring religious resources in Canada, making it more convenient and reinforcing the element of service at the core of our relationship with the Canadian Church.

CONCLUSION

Publishing in these times is not for the weak of heart, as we've seen. While the new terrain has been challenging, Novalis has been able to maintain its financial viability and market share in Canada. The battle is not yet won, and there are scars, but Novalis continues in its original mission to serve the people of God in Canada with affordable, accessible resources to help them nurture and deepen their faith.

ROBIN BAIRD-SMITH

Religious Book Publishing

"I object to publishers. The one thing they have taught me is to do without them. They combine commercial rascality with artistic touchiness with artistic pettiness, without being either good business men or fine judges of literature."

—GEORGE BERNARD SHAW

I STARTED MY FIRST job in book publishing on September 16, 1968. My father said I should not accept a salary of less than 900 (yes, nine hundred) UKP a year and that was precisely what I was offered and accepted. The publishing house was recently founded and was called Darton, Longman and Todd. It still exists and flourishes all these years on. The main mission of the house was to publish religious books—Bibles, theology, liturgical books, patristics, and spirituality. It was in the latter field that I had my early successes and in a *Church Times* survey of religious publishing in 1972 I was described as Robin "spirituality" Baird-Smith. I launched new writers like the Russian Orthodox Anthony Bloom, Rabbi Lionel Blue (who went on to be a star of stage and screen), Carlo Carretto, and Rowan Williams (later to become Archbishop of Canterbury). At this time, I had a strong sense of being closely in touch with our readers, the purchasers of our books. There seemed to be a direct correlation between the quality and the success of the books. To a certain extent this seems to have been lost, for reasons that I will explain.

The most important thing to a book's success was the power of the media. Reviews in the religious press were really powerful. They published on Friday and on Monday I would rush into the office to see the orders rolling in. At ten to eight every Sunday morning, there was a slot on BBC Radio called "The Sunday Reading" (since abolished). This lasted five minutes and consisted of an extract from a spiritual book. When we had a book being read, the effect was electric. Orders poured in. I felt there was something in the then collective unconscious that showed a thirst for transcendence. After all these were the years after the Death of God theology, of *Honest to God* and of writers like Harvey Cox. But these were also the years immediately following the Second Vatican Council (1962–1965). Pope John XXIII had initiated the Council, which carried on after his death and was finally closed by his successor Pope Paul VI. It was a time of real ferment in the Catholic Church. Pope John XXIII had declared that he wished to open the windows of the Catholic Church to the outside world and the fresh air that blew in allowed a whole raft of theologians to write and publish with freedom. Mention should be made of Karl Rahner, Yves Congar, Edward Schillebeeckx, and Hans Küng. Attending the Frankfurt Book Fair became unusually exciting for English-language publishers who were fighting to acquire the book rights of these progressive, liberal, and reforming theologians. My German was just good enough that I could visit German publishers and enquire "Haben Sie eine kleine Rahner?" We snapped up the rights to twenty-four volumes of Karl Rahner's *Theological Investigations*. To crown all this, my publishing house published *The Jerusalem Bible*, the first full Bible published in contemporary English and beating the Anglican *New English Bible* to the post.

In 1979 I moved to become an editorial director at Collins Publishers (subsequently Harper Collins) and for twenty years, I was not concerned in any way with the publishing of religious books. Then, in 1999, I joined the start-up publishing house Continuum, which had a strong interest in publishing religious books and of which I became publishing director. The publishing scene I returned to was dramatically different. Two major developments struck me forcibly—the conglomeration of publishing houses and the Digital Revolution.

It is important to be reminded that most British publishing houses founded in the nineteenth century were most often religious book publishing houses devoted to publishing Bibles and often tracts to promote temperance. These included houses which are still household names—Macmillan,

Methuen, A&C Black, Hodder and Stoughton, T&T Clark, and William Collins. William Collins, for example, opened shop in Cathedral Street in Glasgow in 1819. Collins was a printer as well as a publisher and religious tracts flowed from his presses. Above the entrance to his business were three mottos or words of encouragement.

"If you put your pinkie in a bottle of gin and touch your eye ball you will know what it does to your liver." "Devil trembles when he sees Bibles sold as cheap as these." It was indeed a crusade. But at the bottom under a section called jobs there was a sign that read "Catholics need not apply"!

By the 1960s many of these imprints mentioned above continued to have strong religious book lists but there was also a host of lively small independent houses—SCM Press, Paternoster, Marshall Morgan and Scott, Burns & Oates, and Sheed and Ward, to name only a few.

But this was not to last. In the 1960s it became voguish to invest in publishing houses. Large conglomerates, usually American, moved into the UK and bought small independent publishing houses by the fistful. It was like the frog in the La Fontaine fable. The diminutive animal swallowed more and more and then it burst. In the 1970s an American conglomerate called Crowell Collier Macmillan came and at a sweep, bought five quite unrelated publishing houses. One was the small lively Catholic publisher Geoffrey Chapman. How could it survive in such an environment?

In spite of the fact that this was the year in which E. F. Schumacher published his famous book *Small is Beautiful* the publishing business moved in the reverse direction. Books came to be known so poetically as "product" and selling books became known as "the through put of units."

Salesmen and accountants were in the ascendance and the so-called "creative" departments were in decline. The power of the editor waned. As I have said, most of the small publishers by the turn of the millennium had been gobbled up by Mr. Bertelsman, Mr. Holzspring, and, fate worse than death, Mr. Rupert Murdoch, who had swallowed Collins.

You see, what has happened is that all publishers have become part of a production line for the creation of artifacts for an audience not of readers but of consumers. The book is now a product or a saleable object. Decisions are deferred to marketing departments who in turn defer to chain stores. We come into the world as intelligent creatures, curious and avid for instruction. But it has taken an immense time and effort to dull and stifle our intellectual and aesthetic capabilities, our creative perception. Reading like writing is an art.

How did this affect religious book publishing? The answer is that the same process went on and I became a willing culprit.

As mentioned, in 1999 I became the publishing director of a new publishing house called Continuum. We had offices in London and New York and were financed by a venture capital company that was more interested in growth than profit. The publishing house could not grow sufficiently by organic growth, so we had to hoover up as many religious publishing houses as we could find to buy. We bought the Catholic publishing houses Burns & Oates, Sheed and Ward, and Geoffrey Chapman, the Anglican publishing house Mowbray, and the more academic imprints T&T Clark and Sheffield Academic Press. In time, with the exception of T&T Clark, these venerable houses became obsolete and their character changed. But among the most important books acquired with the acquisitions were the *Church Dogmatics* of Karl Barth, *The History of Philosophy* by Frederick Copleston, and a large number of liturgical books that were published for the Roman Catholic Church in the UK and for the Church of England. All significant backlist fodder.

The second phenomenon that struck me forcibly was the Digital Revolution. This is in many ways a force for good. But it has had two bad consequences.

1. First, the ease with which words can be brought up on screen, played around with, and printed out has meant that the volume of books has increased and thus the quantity of sheer verbiage—a lot of it utterly superfluous verbiage. Most books are just too long today. It is striking that Anthony Bloom, the Russian Orthodox Archbishop in London, has pointed out that there was a Russian peasant who had a locket necklace in which was contained a tiny fragment of a printed Bible. So scarce in Communist Russia were books, especially the Bible, that a tiny fragment of a Bible became hugely significant.

2. Second, the nature of reading has radically changed. For centuries the art of devouring and savoring the printed word was the key to our civilization. People read for enjoyment and understanding—indeed the enjoyment *of* understanding.

There are elements missing from a text viewed on a screen. We talk of "surfing the net." The definition of surfing in this context is "skims the surface of," "rides on the crest of."

And yet the computer is the perfect medium for storing and conveying information. You can now buy two-thirds of all surviving Greek literature up to the time of Alexander the Great on just four easily available disks. This amounts to 3,000,400 words. Isn't it easier to purchase the twelve volumes of the Barth's *Church Dogmatics* as an ebook than struggle back from a bookshop with a stack of clunking volumes? Why should academic essays not be printed first and only on the Internet? A fear of technology is therefore misplaced. In the Digital Revolution, you do not need the ten digits required for holding up a book. And so it is that my publishing house has invested heavily in digital platforms, in what we call "knowledge hubs," and every book is now published simultaneously as a physical book and an ebook. Because of our many acquisitions of publishing houses our backlist is extensive. We have digitized the entire *Church Dogmatics*, the works of major theologians like Rowan Williams, Herbert McCabe, and Edward Schillebeeckx, and we are about to launch a Catholic Theology Hub that will include official Church documents as well as the works of most post-Conciliar Catholic theologians. For better or for worse, the Digital Revolution is here to stay until it itself is replaced. But although this is immensely profitable, as a publisher I no longer feel that I am in touch with the readers of the books I publish, in a manner I described at the outset of this chapter. I also have concerns that the art of reading is diminishing. However, this is not the twilight of the printed word. It is my belief and hope that what I might term "the anti-bookish" movement will drive people back to its birthplace—reading houses like old monastic libraries. Here we will have the luxury of space, we will be able at long last to go back and read in silence. We shall be able once again to go back and engage with the printed word. The revolution in electronic media does not mean that the craft or art (I use the words advisedly) of reading need in any way decline. The Benedictine Abbey, Douai, just outside London, has opened a new modern library, only containing printed books, where members of the public may come and read in complete silence

It is argued that in the world of ubiquitous connectivity, the reader of books will be left behind by those setting out to find meaning through the resources provided by an ever-changing instantaneous media-rich environment. The reading game is about to change forever, we are told. Reading will lose its intellectual and cultural depth. The shift from reading to what one might term "power browsing" (surfing the net) simply diminishes the power of the experience.

But how far we have come? Because of mass education and literacy in the USA and UK almost everyone can read but our imagination and our senses have been dulled by surfing the net, pulp fiction, the desire to imbibe more and more information as fast as possible so we can regurgitate it, pass exams, "succeed." But what is this "irresistible progress" of the absorbing of the written text and what about the cultural revolution it purports to herald? Neuroscientists tell us that we are recasting reading as a "miraculous feat of brain circuitry."

But good reading, and maybe especially good religious book reading, needs attention. The way you focus your attention during learning has a profound impact on the brain's response. For what our new technology permits us to discover is that reading is a demanding activity that shapes you in mind and body. And now in the twenty-first century you see that the problem of reading has shifted to a focus on people's inability to read and many blame the Internet for the loss of the capacity of attention among digitally active readers. An entire generation, we are told, has been diagnosed with an inability to concentrate on the written text. Numerous educational experts allege that it is simply impossible and unrealistic to expect "digital natives" and young people to bother to read a book. And the deficit of their attention span is often blamed on the digital technology and distractions of consumer culture.

According to the American psychologist Andrew Solomon, the rising rates of depression and escalating levels of Alzheimer's disease in the USA can be attributed to the decline of reading. Indeed, he contends the crisis in reading is a crisis in national health. Panics regarding literacy, the reading of literature, the threat to culture posed by texting and social media and online pornography are just some of the problems we can associate with the digital age.

These are complex matters but I am going to conclude by proposing that there is a sense in which St. Benedict and the Benedictine order may once again save our civilization.

The Benedictines teach something called "lectio divina." This is the antidote to everything I have described in the preceding part of this chapter. The Downside Abbey monk David Foster has described "lectio divina" as "Reading with God." It has also been called "godly reading." In his book *Reading with God,* Foster is concerned to bring the riches of the monastic tradition to lay people as they seek to live the Christian life in the modern world. *Lectio divina* is the act of praying with the Bible. It follows St.

Benedict's command to "listen," and attending to the word of God through the printed text helps us to listen to God in a world in which we are surrounded by a cacophony of sound and noise. And, as the US Augustinian Friar Martin Laird has stated so bluntly, "The trouble with modern men and women is that they have cocktail parties going on inside their heads."

Lectio divina is a way of reading. It is not just a way of learning to read prayerfully but to do so with minds and hearts open to God. It is an active kind of reading. We are not just sitting there as passive listeners. But neither are we bombarding God with our own agendas and preoccupations. The traditional stages of *lectio divina* are *lectio, meditatio, oratio,* and *contemplatio.* The person takes the words from the eyes into the mind, repeats them to him or herself, chews over them, and as they begin to be digested, the person responds in prayer, initiating a movement of prayer beyond the words themselves. In this practice, we are in conversation with the writer. We are chewing over the words, digesting them, and responding. This is the complete antidote to that awful occupation "speed reading."

Read a passage slowly, think of the words in relation to each other. Let them sink not just into your mind but into your heart. Let them resonate there. It is essential to read a book as a whole, not to "dip in" or "flick through." We should not expect what we read to have an immediate message, to be immediately grasped and understood.

"Listen," says St. Benedict, "to the words of the master and incline the ear of your heart."

My fear about religious publishing is that the process of conglomeration of lively independent publishing houses is unhealthy. The character and ethos of a publishing house is lost. And the Digital Revolution, though it has immense advantages and is commercially attractive to publishers, is taking people away from the "art" of reading and prevents them from immersing themselves into a printed text. There is no better example than the reading of the Bible and other sacred writings.

This is why I conclude by saying that, yes, once again St. Benedict may save our civilization.

C. JEFFREY WRIGHT

Publishing African American Christians

CHRISTIAN PUBLISHING AND CHRISTIAN books serve the community, the church, the clergy, and the academy by providing resources that shape personal and public Christian life and living. African Americans have been more defined by biblical Christian beliefs than possibly any other group in the country. We look for published books and the Bible to have tangible results so that Christian people will have outwardly defining cultural characteristics, faith, and spiritual practices. One might assume that African Americans, who as a group are among the most engaged in Bible reading and the consumption of Christian books and content, who attend church more, share their faith more, pray more, and give more than any other Christian group in America, would have a significant presence and impact on Christian books and publishing. Consider, too, the fact that the African American community, today at just under 15 percent of the US population, came out of slavery just over 150 years ago, illiterate as a result of American laws and slave codes, which not only made reading illegal for African Americans but also teaching them to read. African Americans were in abject poverty, and their families were scattered by the practices of intentional selling and separating of their families to prevent conspiracies or other efforts to escape slavery. Yet they established more Christian churches over the shortest period of time than any other group in American history. Nearly 40,000 African American churches were established between 1865 and the beginning of the twentieth century throughout the country. Despite this, some of the most influential people in American print history came from the African American community. Oprah Winfrey's Book Club is estimated to have yielded sales of over 55 million books from eighty titles recommended and a slightly fewer number of authors selected by her team between 1996 to 2010. Her most featured author, the late Toni Morrison, had four books selected. Morrison was one of the first African American editors at a major New York publishing house, Random House. She is also perhaps the most awarded author in American history, having won a Presidential Medal of Freedom, a National Humanities medal, a Nobel Prize in Literature, the Pulitzer Prize for Fiction, a National Book Critics Circle Award, and an American Book Award. Although she grew up in a Christian home with a mother who was a devout member of the oldest African American Christian denomination, the African Methodist Episcopal Church (AME), none of her books would be classified as "Christian publishing."

THE AFRICAN AMERICAN CHURCH AND PUBLISHING

In 1773 Phillis Wheatley, an African American slave, wrote a book of poetry, *Poems on Various Subjects, Religious and Moral*, that was notable for being published at all in an era when very few books of any genre were published and certainly none by an enslaved African. The African American community was excluded from the literary life of America. Charles Madison's 600-page history of publishing in the US sums up in one chapter all American publishing up until 1865 and the reality is that there was not much published in America for any community, much less the African American. Until emancipation by law, African Americans could not participate in either the production or purchasing of books and the business of publishing. Indeed, until that moment they did not have the ability to earn money, or obtain an education, and until the end of slavery in 1865 there was literally no leisure time to read.

After emancipation the critical institution of the church gave birth to a community of faith that produced, read, and studied Christian books, as well as to a promotion and distribution system that could facilitate the process. One of the first and eventually one of the largest businesses established in the post-Civil War-era South was the Sunday School Publishing Board of the National Baptist Convention, headquartered in Nashville, Tennessee. This enterprise built an eight-story building that still stands in the center of downtown Nashville and became the commercial center of the largest African American denomination. It was the first national business entity serving African Americans around the country. State Baptist conventions pooled their resources and built this business to support the thousands of new churches that were being established, providing published resources as well as church furniture, offering plates, and everything else needed to start and establish a church. The published resources needed to do small group Bible study and Sunday school were the central focus, along with hymnals and prayer books, a need that was further encouraged during this period for all churches because of the growth of the national Sunday school movement, the Chautauqua movement, and the encouragement of public Christian education. Rev. R. H. Boyd, the entrepreneurial pastor who led the Sunday School Publishing Board, saw this commercial potential and the denomination split over his effort to maintain his family's control of the publishing house. To this day, the R. H. Boyd Company and the affiliated Sunday School Publishing Board of the National Missionary Baptist Convention remain in his family, five generations later, and is one of the oldest multigenerational family-run companies in America. Connecting publishing activity to church activity did not start in the African American community, of course, but it is interesting to note that the emergence of the Sunday School Publishing Board and the African American church, along with the development of nationally distributed Sunday school publishing for the Southern Baptist Convention, occurred during this same period from 1865 to the beginning of the twentieth century.

The Reconstruction period was also followed by the development of independent (non-denominationally connected) Christian publishers including Standard Publishing, David C. Cook, Moody Publishing, and Union Gospel Press, companies founded by Christian evangelists, entrepreneurs, and missionaries who saw the opportunity for resources created apart from the control of the denominations. These companies would serve the African American church and the emerging non-denominationally affiliated churches being founded across the country. Individual consumers were also a customer base, since for most of the companies the main products were small group Bible study guides and other resources for Christian education and Sunday schools.

THE URBAN MINISTRIES INCORPORATED STORY

It was from this group of independent Christian publishers that later included Scripture Press, a company founded in 1932 by husband and wife Victory and Bernice Cory, that Dr. Melvin Banks, Sr., got the vision in 1969 to start an independent African American Christian publisher. Banks saw the need for specifically contextual resources, particularly with stories, history, and images to which the African American community could relate. Ironically, in the nearly one hundred years of Christian publishing by African American denominational publishing houses, a Black community intent on fitting into the mainstream of American life downplayed and diminished the cultural aspects of African American Christianity. Some viewed Black culture as inferior to white culture or as a folk tradition that, in the climate of a rapidly industrializing and educated America, seemed to be a less excellent and less desired culture and worldview. But by the 1960s the Black Power movement and the civil rights movement clashed in a fundamental way that had profound implications for Dr. Banks and African American Christian publishing.

Banks had moved from Birmingham, Alabama to Chicago to study at Moody Bible Institute and eventually attended Wheaton College, where he earned two bachelor's degrees and a master's degree with the intention of returning to the South to start a Bible school. He describes taking a job at Scripture Press as a decision he did not want to make but ultimately made as the result of an argument that he lost with God about where he could best serve his people.

Scripture Press had an interest in reaching the Black community with their books and other products but had no intention of risking their corporate and business reputation serving the African American market in any open and obvious way like changing the content or the color of the resources they created. It was thought that it would clearly offend their Southern constituents during this era of racial polarization, the civil rights struggle, and the culture war embroiling southern whites who made up the majority of their business in the Bible Belt states. Meanwhile, the newly energized African American market was being divided by the Black Power movement's labeling Christianity as a "white man's religion."

Inteen Magazine launched in 1970, from Banks's new company, Urban Ministries, Inc. (UMI), was an African American Christian publishing breakthrough. It was introduced around the same time as two other new

African American audience-focused magazines were launched: *Essence* magazine became the first magazine targeting African American women, while *Black Enterprise* magazine focused on African American entrepreneurs and corporate executives. What Dr. Banks did in creating literature, magazines, and books for the African American Christian consumer and churches was unique—finally a people more committed to their faith than any other group had published resources that affirmed their identity and their presence in the story of the Bible.

Some participation and support of the established Christian publishing industry in the UMI launch was also helpful. Dr. Kenneth Taylor, the creator of the Living Bible who was leading a relatively new independent Christian publishing company that he founded, Tyndale House, contributed. There was support from Scripture Press, where Banks had worked, and from the Zondervan Publishing company, which contributed financially and whose executives served on the board. Those relationships did not last long and UMI became a solely African American-led effort.

The UMI product line expanded throughout the 1980s to include publications for six age levels, so that a church could use the products as its Sunday school or Christian education curriculum for the entire church. A series of leadership development books were also published and adult participation in Vacation Bible School presented the opportunity to publish books for this audience. The company also produced video products to complement its printed literature. UMI joined the Evangelical Christian Publishers Association (ECPA) in 1994 and UMI products became a key part of the product offerings for the emerging African American retailers who started the Christian African American Booksellers Association (CAABA) in 1992. In 1994 Dr. Banks convinced me to leave New York and the security of a Fortune 500 corporate vice president's position to become president of UMI. This was a critical time both because UMI had reached the limit of its ability to grow without additional capital and because, after twenty-five years, Dr. Banks was reaching the limit of his own energy to move the company forward. New ideas, new people, and a commitment to technology to grow the company were needed.

One of the first examples of new corporate culture influencing the trajectory of UMI came in 1996. Michael Jordan was at his peak winning championships with the Chicago Bulls basketball team and inspiring the growth and emergence of the sport as a global industry. Spectacular play, a winning smile, and business savvy changed the sport but also influenced

Christian publishing. Jordan's mother Delores Jordan published a book with Harper Collins called *Family First*. Although not explicitly a Christian title, the Christian principles that Mrs. Jordan used to raise Michael and her other children were evident in her book. UMI was able to show the power of the African American church community as a distribution channel for Christian books by developing a small group study guide for the book, which allowed it to be used in church settings for Bible study, selling tens of thousands of copies as a result. UMI continued to grow its distribution by serving the publishing needs of more than 40,000 African American churches and publishing a few book titles a year that sold large volumes because they were used in adult Bible study classes. The company also became the publisher for nearly a dozen African American denominations that wanted to have the unique benefits of highly contextual resources combined with their denomination's identity in the books. Direct distribution to churches kept UMI from failure when many of the general market Christian publishers serving churches suffered because they depended primarily on distribution of their products through the thousands of Christian bookstores around the nation. These companies faced a different kind of social transformation when Amazon became the number one seller of books, leading to the near demise of an entire industry of Christian book and retail stores. Over the years, Sunday school attendance declined in mainline churches, and many regional and national Christian education conferences ended. This led to the sale or closure of many of the independent publishers in the industry, including Scripture Press, where Dr. Banks got his start. UMI has continued to thrive serving the African American church market with direct sales to churches and to denominations while the demise of the Christian bookstore has continued to impact general market publishers.

CLERGY AND ACADEMIC PUBLISHING

Perhaps the most critical omission in Christian publishing is of resources available to African American pastors, scholars, and professors. Like publishing for the Christian community or for churches, Christian publishing for pastors and the academy has been a story of exclusion, omission, and denial. If African Americans were excluded from participation in the literary life of America before 1865 it was even more true for those who might aspire to publish to serve pastors, teachers, and others who wanted to instruct this group. Of course African American admission to institutions of higher learning was virtually nonexistent before 1865. It is estimated that there were only around forty African Americans with college degrees in the entire country before the end of the Civil War. After the war, over one hundred colleges and universities were founded specifically to educate African Americans, and thus arose a need for materials that the teachers serving in those institutions could use.

Though several of the historically Black seminaries, colleges, and universities were initially set up to train pastors and clergy, the resources were adopted from mainstream schools, authors, and publishers. There was no company for African American academics to publish their works and very few books were published by the established academic publishers or academic divisions of the Christian publishing houses for this market. Sadly, this continues to be the case today. It should be noted though that the liberation theology works of the late Dr. James Cone of Union Theological Seminary, and his students and mentees, are the major exception, but these works were published by the Catholic publisher Orbis Books, the publishing arm of the Maryknoll Fathers and Brothers, a publisher not generally connected to the mainline Christian market. In the 150 years or so since the end of slavery in America there has yet to be established a significant body of work by theologians and graduate school professors to serve the many thousands of African American churches. In fact, one recent study shows that today more Christians live in Africa than any other single continent. A number of important publishing and book distribution efforts are underway in Africa, including the publishing work of Oasis International with their Africa Study Bible, the literature distribution efforts of David C. Cook globally, and the increasing number of self-published authors thanks to Amazon, but there is largely not a sufficient body of scholarly work to address the unique cultural context of the global African church.

CONCLUSIONS

As Christianity continues its decline and its impact on mainstream American culture and life diminishes, Christian book publishing and Christian books are challenged to serve African American and other diverse audiences. The opportunity to serve the African American Christian community and other communities of color remains a need and a huge opportunity. Christian content development would ideally start with the work of scholars and academic leaders who can shape the grand themes that ultimately can be expressed both in the pulpit and in popular culture. The challenge to create both the commerce and the culture for African American Christian publishers, one rooted in a well-formed academic tradition, remains. Publishers need to discover and give opportunity to African American academics and professors who can, in turn, create a publishing record that will allow them to emerge into positions of mentorship and leadership in the academy. Their ideas published for the church and ultimately for the consumer could create the next Reformation.

PETER DWYER

Six Decades of Catholic Publishing in the United States

INTRODUCTION

POPE JOHN XXIII CONVENED the Second Vatican Council on October 11, 1962, setting in motion a far-reaching transformation of Catholicism and a scramble for innovation in Catholic books and media. Among many developments, the Council changed the liturgy and invited ordinary Catholics to read Scripture. New prayer books, catechetical programs, music, and art emerged as established publishers and many newcomers responded to these needs in parishes and schools in the United States.

The number of identifiably Catholic book and magazine publishers more than doubled from 1965 to 2000. A few stalwarts—like the personal missal producer Bruce Publishing—faded early in the competition. But most existing publishers survived the shift and grew alongside new companies founded by church organizations and entrepreneurial laypeople. In time, as their founders retired, many of the for-profit startups would be acquired by religious-owned publishers.

Catholic publishing is a robust field encompassing elhi curriculum, parish faith formation programs, ritual books, music, professional ministry resources, biography, spirituality (a vast subfield), academic and scholarly works, apologetics, and even fiction.

There are more than a dozen Catholic publishers owned by religious orders in the US, and another half-dozen founded by Catholic dioceses.

Slightly more than half of these companies, along with a handful of family-owned publishers, predate Vatican II. The Catholic curriculum publisher William H. Sadlier is the oldest Catholic publisher—and the oldest family-owned publisher of any kind in the US, tracing its origin to 1832 in New York City. The two oldest religious-owned publishers, Ave Maria Press and Paulist Press, date to the 1860s.

Liturgical Press, where I have worked for the past thirty years, was founded in 1926 by Virgil Michel, OSB, a Benedictine monk of Saint John's Abbey. Like many religious-owned publishers, Liturgical Press expanded its mission after the Council. Our original focus on liturgical renewal grew to encompass academic, pastoral, and popular works in Scripture, theology, monasticism, spirituality, and liturgy. As has been the case for many religious-owned publishers, our expansion was accomplished through internal product development, outside partnerships, and the acquisition of private for-profit companies.

GROWTH DECADES

Hymnals and personal missals—thick, small books containing Scripture, prayers, and Mass texts—were among the first major publishing businesses disrupted by Vatican II. After the Council, these traditional hardcovers were supplanted by periodical missals—disposable paperback "missalettes" that combined Scripture readings, Mass texts, and music. The periodical form allowed continuous updates as the new rites and new music were published. But what began as a temporary bridge to the new liturgy became permanent. Despite the ecological concerns of the present day, disposable periodical missals still predominate in parishes.

Liturgical Press developed one of the periodical missals that emerged in the 1960s. While it is important to the resiliency of Liturgical Press, our periodical missal has also been in decline since the 1980s. It has steadily lost market share to similar publications from Oregon Catholic Press (OCP) and World Library. Our crucial mistake was failing to recognize when the value proposition for periodical missals shifted from providing the new rites to featuring new music. Meanwhile, OCP and World Library, together with hymnal publisher GIA, acquired rights for most of the music used in Catholic churches in the post-Vatican II era.

Through the late sixties and into the seventies, during the pontificate of Paul VI, the work of implementing the changes of the Council continued at a brisk pace. Publishing was growing and the audience of educated Catholic readers that had emerged in the 1950s responded enthusiastically. Indeed, Vatican II opened to an interested laity the fields of liturgy, ecumenism, and, especially for Catholics, the study of Scripture.

Notable among startups in this period were Liturgy Training Publications, owned by the Archdioceses of Chicago; Twenty-Third Publications, started by Neil and Pat Klepfuehl (now a division of religious-owned Bayard North America); Michael Glazier, Inc. (an imprint of Liturgical Press since 1990); Orbis Books, founded by the Maryknoll order; and the publishing office of the United States Catholic Conference of Bishops.

Catholic Book Publishing, one of the oldest family-owned Catholic companies, and Fireside Catholic Publishing, a 1970s-era startup, built substantial catalogs of Bible editions to serve the growing interest in Scripture. Two other startups in this period broke new ground for access to Scripture and quickly came to dominate their niches: *Word Among Us*, a daily devotional started in 1981 by a Catholic charismatic community, and Little Rock Scripture Study, founded in the mid-seventies by the Diocese of Little Rock, Arkansas.

Little Rock Scripture Study based its programs on book-by-book Bible commentaries published by Liturgical Press. That association led to a partnership that extended for more than thirty-five years, culminating in the purchase of Little Rock by Liturgical Press in the summer of 2019.

JOHN PAUL II, BENEDICT, AND FRANCIS

Each Pope sets a tone and an agenda for the Church, attempting to shape what is discussed and how the time and resources of the local churches are used. The longer the papacy, the more likely it is that a Pope's vision is realized.

With the election of John Paul II in 1978, a more conservative interpretation of Vatican II began to take hold. His long pontificate resulted in a hierarchy of like-minded bishops and cardinals focused, in the West at least, on culture wars and opposition to abortion. This slow but pronounced shift opened new publishing opportunities for conservative Catholic startups: Ignatius Press, Ascension Press, Sophia Institute, and others. The cable TV station EWTN began broadcasting in 1981. Succeeding where the US bishops had failed, Mother Angelica and EWTN built a national television audience—a hegemony it holds to this day. EWTN, Ignatius Press, and

Sophia Institute are neither religious-owned nor privately held. They are, instead, nonprofit organizations with a religious mission.

Also during the pontificate of John Paul II the Vatican published the Catechism of the Catholic Church. A publishing success in its own right— selling more than four million copies just in the United States—the Catechism also triggered the redevelopment of K-12 curricula by more than a dozen publishers over the past two decades.

The final years of John Paul's papacy were overshadowed by the clergy sexual abuse crisis. Though the first abuse cases came to public attention in the late eighties, the scandal really broke into the open in the Archdiocese of Boston in 2002. Catholics of all ages struggled to understand these terrible crimes committed by priests they had trusted, as well as the cover-up conducted by many bishops.

Joseph Ratzinger was elected Pope in 2005, taking the name Benedict XVI. He continued the theological and liturgical reach-back begun by John Paul II. This was not surprising. As head of the Congregation of the Faith under John Paul II, Ratzinger was key to reasserting the authority of the Vatican through doctrinal investigations of theologians, women's religious communities, and seminaries. These efforts produced a chilling effect, causing publishers to proceed with caution. But with Benedict's papacy the Church also entered the age of social media and the ever-increasing divisiveness of ideological factions with the Church.

The dual surprise of Pope Benedict's retirement and the election of Pope Francis in 2013 turned the Church once again back to Vatican II. Francis emphasizes the mission of the Church to witness to and accompany people who live on the periphery of society. Pope Francis is not only open to debate, he encourages it. This posture has freed writers and publishers to pursue topics they had been avoiding or treating with caution.

AMAZON, BOOKSELLING, AND CATHOLIC BOOKS

At its start Amazon was a useful counterbalance to the dominance of big box chains. But the rise of Amazon quickly went from amazing to threatening. Small independent booksellers were especially hard hit, including religious bookstores. But many religious-owned publishers also have direct-to-customer (consumer and institutional) sales that were undercut by Amazon's loss-leader discounting. Increased discoverability for backlist in the Amazon ecosystem was touted as an offset to the loss of margins. The reality is that after all costs of doing business with Amazon are counted, it is an unprofitable relationship for many publishers.

Like religious-owned publishers Liturgy Training Publications, Our Sunday Visitor, Liguori, Franciscan Media, and others, Liturgical Press has always had significant direct-to-customer sales. To protect our direct business as Amazon grew, we began in the late 1990s to develop annual books designed for bulk sales to parishes—a difficult transaction for Amazon and other online resellers. Though Amazon's share of our book sales continues to rise, the annuals are almost entirely direct-to-customer and now account for 10 percent of our book revenue.

TURBULENT DECADES

The Digital Revolution, which cratered the music industry following the iPod introduction in 2001, began to seriously disrupt book publishing in 2007. The launch that year of the iPhone followed by Amazon's Kindle shifted our digital focus away from the Google Books effort to scan everything in print. Overnight, ebook formats, digital rights, and the shockingly low ebook prices that Amazon introduced to fuel growth in Kindle sales became the new obsession. But another challenge was looming as well.

In late 2008, as the US elections approached, the stock market was in free fall, and bank failures were threatening a new depression for the country and the world. At about that time in presentations to staff and the monastic community that owns us, I began describing the challenges ahead for Liturgical Press and other Catholic publishers in short-, medium-, and long-term categories. Short-term and most urgent was the economy—in a word, survival. Medium-term we had to develop new business models as digital content reshaped publishing. But long-term, and the biggest challenge of all, was the Catholic Church itself.

THE ECONOMY

The great recession of 2008–2009 (officially December 2007–June 2009) was terrible in scope. The repercussions were felt throughout the world and recovery took far longer than two years. The severity of the crisis caused Liturgical Press, and most publishers, religious and secular, to make staff and compensation adjustments. As a first step we froze wages, but eventually we reorganized to streamline operations. Catholic publishers adjusted according to the effect on their customer base. Parishes and schools, like other religious institutions, were especially squeezed by the need to offer more help to parishioners during the recession while donations were falling due to lost jobs.

Publishers had to cut costs in the short term, but we knew that we could not indefinitely cut profitability. We had to grow to stay alive.

THE BUSINESS MODEL

Reshaping the business model of publishing has become much more complex than merely figuring out how to price and sell ebooks. Whereas ebooks represent more than 50 percent of fiction sales, for most Catholic publishers they range from 5 percent to 25 percent of sales depending on the audience and the type of content. For Liturgical Press ebooks have only recently reached 10 percent of sales, but even that masks some underlying changes in the way our customers access content.

Our Michael Glazier Books imprint used to offer large reference works that reliably sold well for many years. Accessing reference information is now often accomplished with online search, making reference works less valuable even in digital editions. As a result, we can no longer afford to publish reference works.

Our publishing approach for homiletics is also changing in response to online resources. Sunday-by-Sunday collections for the three-year Lectionary cycle now sell only one-third as many copies in print and ebook combined as they would have twenty years ago in print alone. Verse-by-verse Scripture commentaries are still in demand, but younger preachers are accessing them in digital collections. And homiletic resources—whether in print or online—compete with a vast and growing trove of free self-published content.

Textbook sales have been falling for several years in religion and the humanities. Though difficult to rank for significance, causes for the decline of textbook sales include fewer students, textbook rental, textbook sharing, ebook access on library platforms, professors and students illegally uploading content for students to access without charge, and students who refuse to buy or even read textbooks.

Monograph sales are under even greater stress. Ebook sales result in lower revenue and shorter, more expensive press runs for print editions. Libraries can no longer afford the rising prices of print editions. For their part, scholars can't keep up with the number of journals and books available. Older scholars are moving to downsize their personal libraries, while younger scholars—far too many on adjunct incomes—can't afford to build a personal library. And increasingly, younger scholars don't see the need to build a personal library when the world is available online.

Though different in the details, similarly complex realities face publishers of elementary and high school curriculum, liturgical resources, adult faith formation programs, music, and spirituality.

Catholic publishing has long had some donor-supported programs or functions. However, over the past twenty years, entrepreneurs like Matthew Kelly (Dynamic Catholic and Wellspring) have driven that model to extraordinary new lengths. The result, for Kelly, is a publishing program that effectively gives books away to parishes and schools.

THE CHURCH

The greatest concerns for Catholic publishers come from the Church. A complex, interrelated set of challenges centered on Catholic identity, governance, and participation frame the future of the Church.

The problems have been building for decades. We have known for more than thirty years that a clergy shortage was slowly strangling parishes. The Catholic research center CARA—my source for the following data—documents a decline of more than 22,000 diocesan and religious order priests in the US between 1970 and 2018.[1] Worse still, only 66 percent of the 25,254 diocesan priests in 2018 were active in ministry, down from 90 percent in 1970. Over the same time span, Catholic population in the US grew from 48 million people to almost 70 million.

The US church has worked to address the clergy shortage with the revival of the permanent diaconate and the more recent development of formation for lay ecclesial ministers. Deacons and lay ministers are important new audiences for publishers, and they can do much of the work in parishes, but only a priest can preside at Eucharist. As a result, dioceses in the US have thus far closed more than 1,000 parishes and combined many more into "area Catholic communities" or clusters of parishes. CARA reports that 3,363 out of 17,007 parishes in 2018 were without a resident priest pastor.

1. CARA.

The clergy shortage alone would have continued to erode participation in the Church, but clergy abuse has shattered the trust of many Catholics. Most thought the worst was behind us when the bishops set up protocols for handling abuse cases in 2002. But we were staggered by the Pennsylvania report in 2018—appalled by the extent and nature of the abuse detailed in the report, and deeply angry with the bishops who covered it up. Indeed, the continuing revelations of abuse hidden by the Church have seriously undercut the moral standing of the bishops and triggered an accelerating exit of Catholics, especially millennials.

There is good news. Concurrent with the slow-motion crisis of too-few clergy and the heinous double crisis of clergy abuse and cover-up by the bishops, the Catholic Church in the US has been rapidly becoming multicultural. In the West and South the Church is growing with immigrant populations from Mexico, Latin America, South America, and various parts of Asia.

The growing multicultural Church is a bright spot demographically. It brings great promise, and a new set of challenges. The Church is still in the early stages of developing effective multicultural models for parish life. And publishing for a multicultural church is complicated by language, dialect, cultural expectations, and varying preferences for media. Spanish, for example, has many dialects. And for recent immigrants especially, there may be significant generational differences in fluency, literacy, and patterns of receiving and sharing information. Among Catholic publishers only those producing liturgical resources in Spanish have thus far found a reliable market.

THE FUTURE

By the fall of 2009, with the economy in a spiral, Liturgical Press decided to develop a new periodical to take the place of our declining periodical missal and to help insulate the company from the predations of Amazon. Launching a new consumer magazine in the worst economy since the 1930s seemed almost foolhardy. And yet, despite the growing dominance of all things digital, what emerged was *Give Us This Day*, a monthly print publication that supports the practice of daily prayer. We began publication in August 2011. Eight years later it has circulation of 100,000 and climbing. It now accounts for one-third of Liturgical Press revenue.

The counterintuitive print-based success of *Give Us This Day* demonstrates a crucial requirement for survival in publishing, Catholic and otherwise. We must understand our audience and work out the right media for each initiative. We cannot simply default to print or digital. The right solution will be an evolving balance of digital text, audio, print, video, social media, and interactive. And that is true for both the product and the marketing.

Shifting into a multimedia way of thinking and doing business is not simply throwing a switch. It is a process of transformation that embraces all of publishing. Transforming our mind-set is crucial, but the most important aspect is finance because our revenue models still depend on print and ebooks. Finance is further impacted because it becomes ever more expensive to track, account for, and audit revenue as it flows through increasingly complex distribution channels.

It seems likely that some form of donor support will be part of the finance solution for most publishers. Fortunately for religious-owned and other nonprofit publishers, Catholic audiences are already accustomed to donating to causes and organizations that align with their interests.

The ability to evolve at the pace of changing media use will determine who survives and prospers in publishing. Of course, Catholic publishers generally face the same challenges and risks as publishers in all fields. Unique to our circumstance are the futures of Church, religious orders, and the spiritual hunger of individuals.

BIBLIOGRAPHY

CARA. Center for Applied Research in the Apostolate. https://cara.georgetown.edu/frequently-requested-church-statistics/.

NORMAN A. HJELM

The Privilege and Perils
of Publishing in a Pluralistic Age

DURING MY SECOND STINT as director and senior editor of Fortress Press
(1980–1984), when its home was in Philadelphia, an event of some importance to "religious publishing" occurred. The board of directors of the
American Book Awards decided to drop from its program any awards in
the category of "Religion/Inspiration." In explaining the elimination of the
category "Religion/Inspiration" from the American Book Awards, the board
said simply that its decision was based on its experience that in this area,
like that of "Current Interest," "there was no clear definition of category."

And I understood that. In that year, 1981, even the list of the house
with which I was associated, a house usually called "denominational," wan-
dered all over the map. That year our lists included a volume on the sociology of the Corinthian church, a neoconservative apology for the ethical
values of democratic capitalism, a piece of Third World spirituality by Dom
Helder Camara, and an interdisciplinary work on the nature of "human
fulfillment." We were the house that, together with Concordia in St. Louis,
was beginning to complete the fifty-five volumes of the American Edition
of Luther's Works, and we were about to begin *Hermeneia—A Critical and
Historical Commentary on the Bible*, a series that is still running.

Add to this miscellany the offerings of other publishers—from Eastern
mysticism to questions raised for religion by the digital age, from the certainties of American evangelicalism to the confusions of Joel Osteen (it was
Richard Bach of *Jonathan Livingstone Seagull* fame in the 1980s)—and one
would indeed be justified in concluding that there is "no clear definition

of the category 'religious books.'" Even more, one must acknowledge that authors who are not to be called "religious writers"—as, for example, Marilynne Robinson or Christian Wiman—often provide the greatest illumination on the themes of faith and doubt and this only complicates the issue.[1]

What is "religious publishing" today? This is an important question with respect to the American religious publishing landscape and one that is unlikely to be answered in a decisive manner any time soon. Publishers will themselves continue to shape their lists in accordance with the needs and traditions of their houses, and to a large extent the presence of a title on a particular list will be justification enough for the label "religious book." Authors, sellers, and readers are, to be sure, at the center of the picture: they create, deal with, and—most importantly—read books. But the light flashes red or green in the offices of the publishers.

Of course, the criteria used by religious publishers in shaping their lists vary: for commercial publishers who have a religious list the chief factor must be economic; for some private publishers, frequently of an evangelical persuasion, it will be the propagation of a particular point of view—political and social as well as theological; for some denominational houses the criterion will be that of service to a readily identifiable community; for others it will be something as broad as "ecumenical and theological" significance; for most publishers it will doubtlessly be a combination of all these elements.

In what follows I propose not to define a category for anything like the American Book Awards, but, rather, simply to present several convictions that might help identify the criteria by which religious publishers make their decisions, how they shape their lists. Moreover, in the conviction that the age of Gutenberg is not over, what follows are really personal reflections on matters of content, professional process, and vocation. My intention is not to forecast the likelihood or unlikelihood of prosperity for religious publishing in the future—economic or cultural. Nor is it to speculate about the prospects of book publishing in relation to other media, chiefly electronic. Rather, these reflections—convictions, if you will—are meant to be

---

1. I am pleased, in illustration of this point, to have recently come across a fine study by Richard Harries, retired bishop of Oxford, *Haunted by Christ: Modern Writers and the Struggle for Faith* (2018). Rowan Williams, now of Magdalene College, Cambridge, has said of this work, "Richard Harries shares with us his reading of many of the great writers of modernity, inviting us to attend with him to their wrestling with the hardest questions of human existence before God—and sometimes before the apparent absence of God."

suggestive of the issues which must be faced if responsible religious publishing is to have any impact on our common life at all.

When I came to Fortress Press at the end of 1962 I had no idea as to what I was getting into. I began as an editor with some theological background and, to be honest, my aim was ultimately to complete a doctorate —perhaps regarding the accomplishment of the great Swedish theologian Gustaf Aulén—in order to settle down teaching undergraduates. A bishop of my church thought similarly and he negotiated a job that would surely allow me to pursue my studies. He and I were both wrong. And, moreover, I soon fell in love with books and the publishing of books. Nearly twenty-five years were spent at Fortress Press. And in what is laughingly called "retirement" I spent more years as a consultant to William Eerdmans, president of the firm that bears his name, very much part-time.

In all of this, I came to feel strongly that the kind of publishing to which Fortress Press was called occupied an essential place in *the theological and ecumenical vocation of the church.* We regarded ourselves as being in partnership with the theological community of the church(es)—individuals and institutions. Questions, answers, publishing decisions—in all of this we approached our work while looking through the lens of the theological tradition. I, a Lutheran, am personally quite able to accept the definition offered by Karl Barth in *Dogmatics in Outline*: "Dogmatics [i.e., systematic theology] is the science in which the Church, in accordance with the state of its knowledge at different times, takes account of the content of its proclamation critically, that is, by the standard of Holy Scripture and under the guidance of its Confessions."[2]

By "lens of the theological tradition" I do not mean that of a particular denominational tradition. At Fortress Press we combined theological publishing in the service of the wider Lutheran community with the explication of serious questions and positions that came from other backgrounds. We held this to be inherent in our ecumenical commitment. Perhaps one, to me unforgettable, experience will typify the attitude we developed, an experience that changed things for the press.

During my initial years at Fortress Press the staff was required to present publication proposals to the Board of Publication of the Lutheran Church in America for approval. In hopes of such approval, we presented a series entitled "Lives of Jesus." This was to be a series of key lives of Jesus from the history of theology—the seminal work of such scholars as David

2. Barth, *Dogmatics in Outline*, 9.

Friedrich Strauss, Friedrich Schleiermacher, Shailer Matthews, and others was to be included. Professor Leander Keck, then at Vanderbilt University, was the general editor of the series. The first volume presented to the board was Hermann Samuel Reimarus (1694–1768), *Fragments*. The proposal turned out to be contentious. When one member of the board decried Remeirus and claimed that he had been around long before the advent of this "modernist theology," we knew that things had to change. The board at its next meeting received a brilliant statement on the responsibility for such publication by the church from Professor Keck and gave the responsibility for decision-making to the staff. *Fragments* was published in 1970.

In addition to seeing its vocation as primarily theological, it became apparent to Fortress Press that the background for serious religious/theological publishing was the inescapable reality of *pluralism*. Whether one looks at the market for books, the background of authors, or the situations of religious institutions, no sweeping generalizations like "this is the way it is—or ought to be" will work. This is the one true fact about culture and society, and increasingly it has come to describe the situation in which church, synagogue, and mosque live.

For religious publishing this means several things. First, that pluralism itself is a subject that must be a concern of "religious books," requiring sharp sociological, theological, ecclesial, and cultural insight. Second, it means that the readers—the market—of religious books are not to be viewed in any parochial way as holding to uniform beliefs or values. For those publishers whose charter comes from a specific religious institution, a new set of responsibilities is necessary, usually a broadening of focus. And for those publishers who seem so easily to identify a specific religious or moral point of view with absolute positions—personal, social, theological, or institutional—a radical shift in outlook is required.

This importance of pluralism became clear to me, as director of the press, when I first attended a meeting of the official Lutheran-Jewish Dialogue in the late 1960s. Subsequently we entered that group of publishers who aimed a key part of their program at the question of Jewish-Christian relations—to be seen biblically, historically, theologically, and pluralistically culturally. Books such as the one from that mentioned dialogue, *Speaking of God Today: Jews and Lutherans in Conversation,* edited by Marc Tanenbaum and Paul Opsahl (1974), *Anti-Semitism in the New Testament?* by Rabbi Samuel Sandmel (1978), *The Roots of Anti-Semitism* by Heiko Obermann

(1981), *Tractate on the Jews: The Significance of Judaism for Christian Faith* by Franz Mussner (1984), and a number of others resulted.

These reflections are also grounded in the conviction that the theological framework for serious religious publishing must be radically *ecumenical*. Of late this has not been a particularly popular dimension of the religious life, especially among some mainline institutions, and indeed in some quarters there are signs of theological and social retrenchment such as to lead to the suspicion that ecumenism is a thing of the past. In a time when *survival* is perhaps the primary concern of American religious institutions, what is essential for the perseverance of those institutions is the development of an expanded ecumenical framework. Publishing decisions in the area of theology and the academic study of religion will either facilitate or block that expansion. Tests of validity and judgment will be on the basis of content itself and not institutional affiliation.

For Christians, I am convinced, what is required is to put the ideal of "evangelical catholicity" into flesh and blood bringing a newly shaped consciousness of unity into reality.[3] Books of theology and spirituality, books of instruction and ethical concern are to be written by authors who, like their readers, stand on bases broader than institutional or denominational loyalty. To put things differently, this new framework will mean "being increasingly oriented to the world-*Oikumene,* with its different regions and religions, ideologies and sciences, and with all the political and social problems involved . . ."[4] A radical commitment to the unity of "the whole inhabited earth" against the background of secular and religious pluralism will mark the serious religious book of the future.

To conclude my reflections on the category "religious books," let me simply state that serious religious publishing needs to focus on *a new context for the individual reader.* Inasmuch as my own experience has been largely with academic monographs and texts, I cannot claim much authority for the following remarks, but they do represent an attempt to deal with crucial elements that have marked the course of religious publishing in America.

Two kinds of books that are generally placed under the heading "religious books" and that over recent decades have attained considerable

3. What is perhaps the best explication of "evangelical catholicity" has, sadly, never appeared in English. I refer to the work of the Swedish theologian Sven-Eric Brodd in *Evangelisk och katolicitet: Ett stadium av innehåll och function under 1800- och 1900-talen* [*Evangelical and Catholicity: A Study of Content and Function in the 19th and 20th Centuries*] (1982).

4. Hans Küng; the author could not locate this citation.

popularity are "self-help" books and books of "spirituality." To put it bluntly, these classifications are badly in need of being recast.

"Self-help" is itself a shaky religious category, yet under its guise countless atrocities have been inflicted on the American reading public by pandering publishers. Religious publishers, often thinking they know a good thing when they see one, have jumped aboard with their own brands of second-rate psychology veneered with cheap piety or biblical phraseology—"How to Combine Prayer, Praise and the Spiritual with Work, Play and the Physical" as the ad copy reads. And books of "spirituality" have appeared by the dozens marked, to be sure, by authentic classics and first-rate theology and anthropology, but results have more often than not been imitative, individualistic, and arcane.

Can self-help books of authentic theological strength be developed? Books that will stress the genuine yet ambiguous possibilities for human life inherent in religious faith in a complicated world? Books which will foster personal maturity while at the same time bringing to life religious realities such as grace, ultimate dependence, forgiveness, and obedience? Can books of spirituality escape the irrelevancies of those books that used to be described as "personal devotion"? Can books for the life of prayer and worship be set firmly within a context of social and ethical responsibility without succumbing to every trend of mindless relativism? Religious books, after all, are meant to be read by persons. The test for religious publishers will largely be formed by their perceptions of authentic personhood within the world we know. Only such books will help.

A second kind of issue has to do with marketing realities. The control of American bookselling by monster entities like Amazon has also turned the world of publishing on its head. On the one hand, of publishers, even small ones, higher degrees of flexibility are required: their books are available and old modes of marketing—advertising, direct mail, the use of sales forces—are increasingly that, old. Increased awareness of the antiquities of previous methods of discounting, freight, and media promotion is required and the development of new and imaginative methods are also required if even a small number of worthy titles are to get beyond the ghetto of religious outlets.

Religious publishers, I have come to think, must increasingly approach their market(s) as an institutional one rather than a retail one. Clergy—priests, pastors, rabbis—as well as teachers and academics must be convinced that books (and studying and reading) are a part of their vocation.

Universities and theological seminaries must be joined by parishes and synagogues as outlets for various types of books. It is more important for religious publishers to secure adoption of their books by colleges and seminaries and institutional programs affiliated with, say, Confraternities of Christian Doctrine, than to place expensive but nonproductive advertisements in *The New York Times.*

Finally, let these reminiscences and ruminations emphasize that religious publishing must increasingly and with awareness be permeated with the spirit of partnership. And this, I suppose, is the burden of all these remarks. Religious publishing is a totally cooperative enterprise, even if in arrogance or ignorance publishers often fail to acknowledge it. The publisher, if committed to an exciting and important vocation, will recognize that in relation to the world of crucial ideas she or he stands alongside the author. The book is to the idea much as the form is to the substance. The publisher, furthermore, will recognize that in relation to the world of religious institutions she or he often operates, as one church leader has said, as a "functional bishop." The decision of what to publish or what not to publish helps shape communities, form convictions, and determine action. And the publisher will recognize that in relation to the reader—who emphatically is not to be considered the "consumer" in an enterprise which is not to be labeled an "industry"—he or she bears the greatest responsibility of all: that of making available through words, worthy or unworthy, those ideas or deeds that ennoble or debase human life. The responsibility is great and ours is a vocation of partnership.

To have been asked, albeit so briefly, to reflect on the vocation of religious publishing is obviously to have been asked to think again about the nature and significance of time. Time in relation to the world of words, of ideas, even of the most basic human commitments. When the great German publisher Peter Suhrkamp died in 1959, to be succeeded at the helm of the major firm Suhrkamp Verlag by Peter Unseld, the Nobel Laureate Herman Hesse wrote to him with eloquence and in a way that can be applied to the overall concern of this essay: "The publisher must move 'with the times,' as people say, yet he should not simply follow the fashions of the times but also be able to resist them when they are undesirable. The function, the very breathing in and out, of a good publisher consists of accommodation and critical resistance. This is the kind you should be."[5]

5. Unseld, *The Author,* 37, cf. also 78.

As with most things of importance, to reflect on the vocation of religious publishing is not to predict or dream. It is, rather, to discern the shape of those issues that will make hopeful and confident entry into that vocation possible. With good partners the religious publisher can walk straight ahead.

BIBLIOGRAPHY

Barth, Karl. *Dogmatics in Outline*. Translated by G. T. Thomson. New York: Philosophical Library, 1949.

Brodd, Sven-Eric. *Evangelisk och katolicitet: Ett stadium av innehåll och function under 1800- och 1900-talen [Evangelical and Catholicity: A Study of Content and Function in the 19th and 20th Centuries]*. Lund: C. W. K. Gleerup, 1982.

Harries, Richard. *Haunted by Christ: Modern Writers and the Struggle for Faith*. London: SPCK, 2018.

Unseld, Siegfried. *The Author and His Publisher*. Translated by Hunter Hannum and Hildegqrde Hannum. Chicago: University of Chicago Press, 1980.

RICHARD BROWN

Publishing as Service:
The Moral Traditions Book Series
and Communities of Practice

IN THE EARLY 1990s John Langan, SJ, a professor of philosophy at Georgetown University and the then-chair of the Georgetown University Press
advisory board, approached an associate professor at Weston Jesuit School
of Theology to discuss the prospect of a book series in Christian ethics.
That professor, James F. Keenan, SJ, currently Canisius Professor and director of the Jesuit Institute at Boston College, set out to establish what would
become the most important series in the field: Moral Arguments and Moral
Traditions, later shortened to Moral Traditions. That series, now consisting
of more than sixty books on a range of topics by a diverse list of outstanding
scholars, has reflected critical developments in Catholic moral theology.
Even more, the series illuminates the continuing relevance and significance
of the printed word as a means of not only influencing how a field is studied
and taught but how publishing and books can contribute to and sustain a
community of practice.

In this brief essay I will discuss the Moral Traditions series and why it
remains an exemplary model of scholarly publishing: not only advancing
intellectual debates, but also speaking to policy and policy making. I will
also discuss criteria of successful scholarly books series, and the importance of publishing book series for communities of practice.

A BRIEF HISTORY

The aims of the Moral Traditions series were established at its creation and drive the series today: to examine traditions, and the long-standing claims that fundamental moral theology and Christian social ethics make on human beings and communities today. Some books in the series scrutinize key concepts from significant writers whose works continue to influence contemporary Christian ethics. Others study whether a significant insight long latent in moral traditions deserves fuller recognition. Still others examine how particular communities once shaped by key practices now look to redefine their ethical commitments in a more pressing world. And finally, some compare elements of other moral traditions with Christian ones.[1]

The first book in the series appeared in 1995: Stephen J. Pope's *The Evolution of Altruism and the Ordering of Love*. Over the next several years a wave of books emerged. Many focused on Catholic moral theology and the virtues; others looked outside the United States at intellectual traditions and trends in Europe; several others focused on social problems, such as war and peace, poverty, immigration, welfare, gender and sexuality, and issues in medicine and bioethics. Some were highly specialized monographs examining specific thinkers, particularly Thomas Aquinas, whose influence on Catholic moral and fundamental theology, as well as Christian ethics, continues to be limitless. Perhaps one of the series' most ambitious projects was *The Ethics of Aquinas*, released in 2002. Edited by Stephen J. Pope, this oversized, 512-page anthology included contributions from twenty-eight scholars from around the globe and continues to serve as the authoritative resource on the subject.

While most of the early books in the series were written by men, women scholars made critical and innovative contributions and, over time, the series reflected a stronger and more intentional gender balance. One such contribution was Cristina Traina's *Feminist Ethics and Natural Law* (1999), which proposed a challenging and controversial thesis: that a truly Thomistic natural law ethic provided a much-needed holistic foundation for contemporary feminist ethics.

In 2002 another innovative volume appeared that captured important developments in the field, *Medicine and the Ethics of Care*, edited by Diana Fritz Cates and Paul Lauritzen. The following year Maura Ryan's widely

---

1. See http://press.georgetown.edu/MoralTraditions.

reviewed *Ethics and Economics of Assisted Reproduction: The Cost of Longing* analyzed the intersections of ethical theory and economic justice and medical ethics and public policy analysis, situating the issue of assisted reproduction not as an individual decision but within the context of the common good.

This attention to medicine and bioethics continued in the years ahead, resulting in one of the landmark publications in the series: Lisa Sowle Cahill's *Theological Bioethics: Participation, Justice, and Change.* Cahill, a mentor of many of the younger authors in the series, is J. Donald Monan Professor of Theology at Boston College and former president of the Society of Christian Ethics and the Catholic Theological Society of America. Winner of the 2006 Catholic Press Association best book in theology, *Theological Bioethics* contended that a legitimately "participatory" bioethics must begin with access to health care, underscoring the series' attention to addressing policy. Cahill's book became one of the best-selling volumes in the series and on the Georgetown University Press list.[2]

Perhaps the most well-known author in the series is Charles Curran, a Catholic priest and the Elizabeth Scurlock Professor at Southern Methodist University. Curran has written nine books in the series and is, arguably, the most important figure in the field of Catholic moral theology—though he has been unable to teach at a Catholic institution for more than thirty years. Curran's remarkable saga has been documented in his memoir, *Loyal Dissent: Memoir of a Catholic Theologian.*[3] In 1986, the Vatican declared that Curran, a tenured professor, could no longer teach theology at The Catholic University of America. Curran's lawsuit against the University for wrongful dismissal and breach of contract failed, despite strong support from the Association of American Professors. It was the Sacred Congregation for the Doctrine of the Faith, headed by then-Cardinal Joseph Ratzinger (later Pope Benedict XVI), that rejected Curran's theological and ethical views regarding divorce, artificial contraception, masturbation, premarital intercourse, and "homosexual acts."[4] Winding up at SMU, Curran remains

---

2. Many volumes in the series focus on policy, including *United States Welfare Policy: A Catholic Response* (2008) by Tom Massaro, SJ; *Kinship across Borders: A Christian Ethic of Immigration* (2014) by Kristin Heyer; and *Consumer Ethics in a Global Economy: How Buying Here Causes Injustice There* (2019) by Daniel K. Finn.

3. http://press.georgetown.edu/book/georgetown/loyal-dissent.

4. https://www.aaup.org/NR/rdonlyres/9CA4679F-7BC7-4AD7-BA37-0C1B00AE-BAA1/0/CatholicUUSA.pdf.

one of the most prolific scholars in the field; his most recent book, *Diverse Voices in Modern U.S. Moral Theology,* was published in 2019.[5]

One of the happiest moments in the history of the Moral Traditions series was the publication of a *Festschrift* for Curran: *A Call to Fidelity: On the Moral Theology of Charles E. Curran* (2002).[6] Edited by James J. Walter, Timothy E. O'Connell, and Thomas A. Shannon, the book featured fourteen essays from an array of celebrated moral theologians (as well as one from Protestant ethicist James Gustafson, who referred to Curran as an "ecumenical theologian par excellence"), all of whom celebrated the enormous influence of Curran on the field and the academy and the Church.

Other books in the Moral Traditions series also generated controversy within the Roman Catholic Church. One in particular was *The Sexual Person: Toward a Renewed Catholic Anthropology* (2008) by Todd A. Salzmann and Michael G. Lawler, both of Creighton University, a Jesuit institution. The reviews poured in, and the book was lauded as "brilliant" by a reviewer in the Jesuit journal *Theological Studies.* But the response from the Church hierarchy was decidedly negative. Lawler and Salzman were rebuked by the Committee on Doctrine of the U.S. Conference of Catholic Bishops for "defending the moral legitimacy of homosexuality, contraception, premarital sex and other hot-button issues in sexual ethics."[7] The Committee on Doctrine, then chaired by the Archbishop of Washington, Donald Wuerl,[8] explained in a twenty-four page response that Salzman and Lawler's work

5. As the then-director of Georgetown University Press I made it a point to alert the board chair of Curran's books prior to publication, and the response I received was consistent: If the book has passed peer review, if it makes an intellectual contribution to the field, and if it fits with editorial vision for the press, move forward. And in fact I recall receiving occasional letters (and later, emails) from disgruntled Catholics unhappy that the press was publishing Curran's work.

6. During my publishing career I have consistently rejected proposals for *Festschriften,* a politically tricky and financially dicey genre. Georgetown University Press had agreed to publish the Curran *Festschrift* before I arrived, and I am relieved I did not have to make that decision.

7. See *National Catholic Reporter's* reporting here: https://www.ncronline.org/news/us-bishops-rebuke-creighton-theologians. Publishers generally love controversial books. I recall watching the book shoot up the Amazon best-seller list in Religion every time the "rebuke" from the U.S. Conference of Catholic Bishops was mentioned in an article. At the same time, I had some anxious moments wondering if the bishops planned to contact the Georgetown University administration to discuss the matter. To my knowledge, they did not.

8. Wuerl resigned from that post in 2018 amid accusations of mishandling child abuse cases during his tenure as bishop of Pittsburgh in the early 2000s.

represented a "radical departure from the Catholic theological tradition."[9] The publisher couldn't have asked for better publicity: when the U.S. Catholic Bishops' response became public the book immediately became one of Amazon's bestselling religion books.

It was the vision, commitment, and intellectual courage of series editor Jim Keenan, SJ that guided Moral Traditions during its first twenty years. Keenan contributed one of the early volumes, coediting *The Context of Casuistry*, and later published numerous books with a variety of religion and commercial publishers. In 2002 he also established an initiative that has brought together thousands of theologians at international meetings, Catholic Theological Ethics in the World Church.[10] But by 2014 Keenan was ready to move on; he stepped down as series editor to focus on other responsibilities. Rather than appoint a single successor, Georgetown University Press named three series editors: Kristin Heyer, then of Santa Clara University; Andrea Vicini, SJ, of Boston College; and David Cloutier of The Catholic University of America.[11] Today the series continues to be productive, with several volumes published in 2019.

PUBLISHING SUCCESS CRITERIA

Why do some book series succeed and others fail? The Moral Traditions series offers an object lesson:[12]

- *Editorial fit*: The series must be a good fit for the scholarly publisher's book list and must reflect editorial priorities; "interesting" books and series that readers wouldn't expect in the catalog may satisfy an acquisitions editor's whim but are risky.[13] Georgetown University Press,

9. See note 7.

10. http://www.catholicethics.com/.

11. Kristin Heyer, who contributed two volumes to the series, was succeeded in 2018 by Darlene Weaver, professor of theology (and soon after associate provost of academic affairs) at Duquesne University.

12. I have worked with dozens of book series during my publishing career, some of which I inherited, some of which I initiated, and some of which I canceled. I put the odds of establishing an enduring, successful book series at 50/50. Like a marriage, such relationships always begin with grand dreams and commitments and intentions. Canceling a series is never pleasant, and in some cases the former series editors have remained bitter toward me ever since. But publishing requires saying no far more often than saying yes.

13. That said, sometimes scholarly publishers must plough new ground—but only if they can occupy an editorial niche not already dominated by other publishers, and only

lodged within a Jesuit, Catholic university, is the right place for such a series.

- *Editorial parameters*: The publisher and the series editors must identify, agree on, and publicize the kinds of issues and topics the series should address; the series must have editorial coherence without predictability. Under Keenan's leadership the series reflected a theologically moderate/progressive approach to moral traditions; as Keenan commented, the series was interested in moral traditions moving forward, not using them to keep members rooted in the past.[14]

- *Publishing commitment*: The publisher must be actively committed to the series by a) scheduling a steady flow of new books, b) mailing out an adequate number of review copies, c) promoting the series through direct mail and social media, and d) exhibiting at key academic conferences. Georgetown University Press has been a consistent presence at the Society of Christian Ethics annual meeting and the Catholic Theological Society of American annual meeting, as well as the larger American Academy of Religion annual meeting.

- *Who cares*?: Who is the audience? Scholars and graduate students? Undergraduates, or the general public, or both? The vast majority of the Moral Traditions volumes are aimed at scholars and grad students and seminaries, as befitting a scholarly publisher. In one case, Julie Hanlon Rubio's *Family Ethics: Practices for Christians* (2010),[15] the target audience was the lay community and adult education groups, but the possibility of classroom adoptions was strong enough to warrant inclusion. [16]

---

if they fully commit to the field or subfield.

14. Email exchange between the author and Keenan, September 25, 2019.

15. The author and I discussed the appropriateness of this volume for the series, considering Paulist Press and other lay-oriented options. But the writing was so crisp and the arguments so important that Jim Keenan, SJ and I agreed that the series could and should accommodate it. That proved to be a good decision.

16. A counter example was an interdisciplinary book series I initiated in human rights. The series produced several good books, but after seven years I canceled it. One major reason was that the academic study of human rights is multifaceted, with a wide range of perspectives: law, philosophy, international affairs, religion, sociology, public health, and so on. There was no single community of practice—there were *multiple* communities, and they didn't necessarily read each other's books.

- *The right series editors*: The series editors must be authorities in the subject matter, of course, but must also be supremely well connected and well respected in their field—and willing to discriminate between publishable projects and nonstarters. Above all, they must consistently generate book projects, season after season.

- *Grooming the next generation*: Scholarly book series should aim for a mix of established stars and ascending lights. Moral Traditions includes the leading figures in the field, such as Charles Curran, Lisa Cahill, David Hollenbach, and Stephen Pope. But throughout its history the series provided a platform for early-career scholars publishing their first books: Maura Ryan, Aaron Stalnaker, Kristin Heyer, Elizabeth Bucar, Andrew Flescher, Cristina Traina, Joe Kotva, Susanne Decrane, and many others, all of whom made a significant impact on the field and who are now mentoring the next crop of scholars.

- *Ongoing communication*: The series editors and the publisher must meet and/or speak regularly to check the progress of the pipeline, that is, manuscripts either under peer review or contracted but not yet published. In addition, the publisher must ensure that, if more than one series editor is involved, the workload is equitable.[17]

- *Sense of community*: On rare occasions a book series takes on a life of its own: authors feel they are a part of a community, not simply another contributor to a sea of books on a shelf. Over time Moral Traditions became widely known as the "Keenan series," which not only revealed Jim Keenan, SJ's influence but also helped with author recruitment and sales. One way that Georgetown University Press tried to create that sense of community was by sponsoring a dinner to honor the Moral Traditions authors at the Society of Christian Ethics (SCE) annual meeting.[18] It was at these dinners that the press brought together members of a community of practice.

17. During my tenure at Georgetown University Press I held working breakfasts with the series editors twice a year: at the Society of Christian Ethics annual meeting and the Catholic Theological Society of American annual meeting. During those meetings we would pore over a spreadsheet of prospects and projects in the pipeline, then make assignments for follow-up. Those were the happiest and most energizing publishing meetings of my year.

18. These dinners typically involved twenty to twenty-two authors and other friends of the press and included spirited discussions about issues in Christian ethics and moral theology, multiple toasts and bottles of wine, and critiques of the SCE's presidential address.

SERVING A COMMUNITY OF PRACTICE

A fundamental strategy for scholarly book publishers is to identify and then integrate themselves into a small number of communities of practice that align with the publisher's editorial program. Communities of practice, a term popularized by anthropologists Jean Lave and Etienne Wenger, are simply groups of people who engage in a process of collective learning in a shared domain or human endeavor. Wegner identifies three characteristics of such groups: a shared commitment and shared competence, in which individuals and groups can learn from each other; joint activities and discussions in order to share information and build relationships; and a shared repertoire of resources, stories, tools, and ways of addressing recurring problems.[19] This is one of the defining characteristics of the Moral Tradition series: it *reflects* the work of a community of practice and also *informs* and *influences* teaching and research in the field.[20] The series itself, in its own small way, helps sustain a community of scholars who are committed to a moral tradition—a commitment that includes advancing intellectual arguments and changing policy. This throws light on an essential purpose of the scholarly publisher: to serve such communities of practice.

In my view scholarly publishers must be clear about *why* they do what they do, because the *why* question is ultimately more important than the books they publish or how they promote them. Scholarly publishers facilitate the production of resources to help scholarly communities of practice advance their teaching, learning, and research—in short, they serve others. Seen in this light, scholarly publishing is a vocation, one that acknowledges fundamental obligations of being human and living in community.[21] Those obligations motivate publishers to get out of bed in the morning and to be vital knowledge organizations that are indispensable to their fields, integral and active partners in the scholarly ecosystem.

This commitment to serving a community of practice is the foundation of the Moral Traditions series, and what makes it a successful and enduring publishing enterprise. Those sixty-three books (and counting) educate, inspire, and help sustain a community of practice. And by serving

19 Wenger-Trayner and Wenger-Trayner, "Introduction."

20. A vigorous discussion within the scholarship around communities of practice is the study of knowledge management, which arose from the sciences with an emphasis on interdisciplinary collaboration but which is also applicable to arts and the humanities. See Handzic and Carlucci, eds., *Knowledge Management*.

21. Brown, "Stakeholders."

this community of authors and practitioners, by fulfilling its vocation, Georgetown University Press serves the common good.[22]

BIBLIOGRAPHY

Allen, John L., Jr. "US Bishops Rebuke Creighton Theologians." *National Catholic Reporter.* https://www.ncronline.org/news/us-bishops-rebuke-creighton-theologians.

Brown, Richard. "Stakeholders, Service, and the Future of University Press Publishing." *Journal of Scholarly Publishing* 44.2 (January 2013) 107–13.

Handzic, Meliha, and Carlucci, Daniela, eds. *Knowledge Management, Arts, and Humanities: Interdisciplinary Approaches and the Benefits of Collaboration.* Springer, 2019. https://link.springer.com/book/10.1007%2F978-3-030-10922-6.

Wenger-Trayner, Etienne, and Beverly Wenger-Trayner. "Introduction to Communities of Practice: A Brief Overview of the Concept and Its Uses." https://wenger-trayner.com/introduction-to-communities-of-practice/.

22. I would like to thank Jim Keenan, SJ and Kristin Heyer for their helpful comments on an earlier draft of this essay.

ANDREW T. LE PEAU

Evangelical Academic Book Publishing: 1970–2020

In March 1991 four editors sat in a small, windowless conference room on the second floor of a building that had been converted from a Buick dealership to serve the needs of a publishing house. The topic of discussion was academic books and whether our publisher should expand in this arena.

Since its early days in the 1940s, the publishing house, InterVarsity Press, had been largely dependent on its sister publishing house, Inter-Varsity Press–UK, for a flow of academic and reference books. The Tyndale Old Testament Commentaries as well as books by scholars such as F. F. Bruce originated in Britain. Occasionally IVP-US had produced original books that were used in the academy, such as Richard Lovelace's *Dynamics of Spiritual Life* or James Sire's *The Universe Next Door*. IVP had even regularly produced an academic catalog as early as the 1970s. But such books were generally ad hoc publications. Then, on that March day, Dan Reid, Jim Hoover, Rodney Clapp, and I met to decide if this was the time for IVP in the US to create a steady, deliberate plan to expand its own academic publishing program.

As we talked, we thought there were several reasons that this might be the time to do so. First, IVP had always been part of a campus ministry (InterVarsity Christian Fellowship) with an ethos that took the university seriously. Second, we saw a more open market than the crowded field of books for the general Christian public. Certainly there were established mainline publishers like Fortress, Abingdon, Orbis, and Westminster John Knox. But only a few evangelical publishers were in the mix in a serious way. Third, we thought IVP could set itself apart from those few by being broadly evangelical rather than largely Reformed or mainline in profile. Fourth, as a team, the four of us had the background and interests to develop such books. Fifth, we saw a large and growing pool of qualified authors teaching at Christian institutions at home and internationally.

Having haphazardly produced a few such titles a year, we decided to begin modestly by aiming for six academic books in 1993 and perhaps ten a year by mid-decade. One positive step came soon after that March 1991 meeting when Rodney Clapp visited with Donald Bloesch, longtime professor of theology at the University of Dubuque Theological Seminary. As a result, from 1992 to 2004 IVP published the seven volumes in Bloesch's systematic theology series, Christian Foundations. Dozens of primary and supplemental texts came soon after in a variety of disciplines including Bible, theology, philosophy, history, and psychology.

Overall the results far exceeded our projections. Within five years we had released seventeen academic books in a single year, and in the first year of the new century, we released thirty-two new titles.[1] Within a few more years academic and reference publishing had grown to 44 percent of IVP's total income. Our presence and prestige also grew at the annual academic gatherings of the Society of Biblical Literature, the Institute for Biblical Research, and the Evangelical Theological Society.

During the 1990s Dan Reid focused most of his attention on what would become a series of ten Bible dictionaries, the first of which, *Dictionary of Jesus and the Gospels,* was published in 1992. These "black dictionaries" (so-called for the black design of the covers) became standards of biblical scholarship that were welcomed well outside evangelicalism, finding homes in the libraries of elite universities and the offices of their faculty.

In 1998 IVP published the first two of what, under Jim Hoover's guidance, would become twelve years later a twenty-nine-volume series that John Wilson of *Books & Culture* called "the most important project in religious publishing at the end of the second millennium." The Ancient Christian Commentary on Scripture (ACCS) would take the most salient comments from the church fathers and arrange them under a paragraph or chapter of Bible text. Over a half million copies were sold of the substantive, hardback volumes.

---

1. Le Peau and Doll, *Heart. Soul. Mind. Strength,* 123.

The ACCS was the most conspicuous example of IVP reaching beyond the borders of evangelicalism. Contributors ranged from evangelical Protestant to mainline Protestant to Catholic to Orthodox. The buyers of volumes were also proportional to how these religious traditions were represented in the general population.

In the twenty-five years following 1991, IVP released over 900 academic and reference books. But a funny thing happened while IVP's program was expanding: so were the academic publishers we identified as also serving our target market, and other publishers entered the arena as well.

EXPANDING PROGRAMS

Zondervan, Baker, and Eerdmans publishing houses share more than Dutch roots and a Grand Rapids address. Their academic growth followed a pattern similar to that of IVP's. They started as booksellers who quickly began publishing books. They were different from IVP in that many of their early books were public domain or out-of-print titles, often from Europe, which they produced alongside some original works.

Zondervan republished multivolume works from J. C. Ryle, Charles Spurgeon, Charles Ellicott, and others in the 1950s. Calvin, Kuyper, and Bavinck showed up in Eerdman's list. Baker also had good success with its many reprints.

In addition, all three along with IVP picked up North American rights to new titles from British publishers including IVP-UK, Paternoster, and others. Longtime editor at Eerdmans, Jon Pott, estimates that in those middle decades of the last century, perhaps one-third of all Eerdmans books originated in Europe.[2] Karl Barth, Jacques Ellul, Gerhard Kittel, Helmut Thielicke, and Thomas Torrance were all in their catalog.

Such books laid a foundation on which US-originated projects could be built. William B. Eerdmans, Jr.'s vision, beginning in the 1960s, opened the door beyond evangelical concerns to a wide range of ecumenical interests.[3] In the subsequent decades Lutheran, Catholic, Orthodox, and Jewish authors would regularly appear in their offerings.

In the 1960s Zondervan published Ronald H. Nash, J. Oliver Buswell, Jr., and J. Barton Payne as well as originating hefty reference books.[4] Rob-

2. Jon Pott in personal interview with the author, April 30, 2019.

3. Ten Harmsel with Van Till, *Eerdmans Century*, 144–45.

4. Ruark, *House of Zondervan*, 91–92.

ert Gundry's standard text *Survey of the New Testament* (now in its fifth edition) was first published in 1970, coincidentally the same year Zondervan released the multimillion bestseller *The Late Great Planet Earth.*

Even so, only in the following decade did Zondervan put its academic program on a consistent footing. Bob DeVries hired Paul Hillman, and together they expanded the list so that by 1980, Zondervan had 275 texts in their backlist accounting for 17 percent of units sold by Zondervan (up from 12.6 percent in 1973).[5]

It wasn't until January 1980, however, that the company hired its first full-time academic editor—Stan Gundry, brother of Robert.[6] Stan had taught at Trinity Evangelical Divinity School as an adjunct and had recently left his position of professor of theology at Moody Bible Institute, where he had been on the textbook advisory committee for Moody Press.

The landmark event that had an immense impact on Zondervan's academic program was publication of the New International Version of the Bible (NIV)—the New Testament in 1973 and the whole Bible in 1978. This stimulated the release of many reference works and commentaries by the company.

The first volumes of the *Expositor's Bible Commentary* based on the NIV were released in the mid-1980s and took nearly fifteen years to complete. Gundry also oversaw the production of a series of companion concordances by Edward Goodrick and John R. Kohlenberger III, and initiated the NIV Application Commentary series.

The NIV also spawned a whole family of Greek- and Hebrew-language study tools, such as the four-volume *NIV Interlinear Hebrew-English Old Testament* edited by Kohlenberger and William Mounce's *Basics of Greek Grammar* (now in its fourth edition).

Baker also began making major moves in the 1980s, publishing a variety of core reference titles such as the two-volume *Baker Encyclopedia of the Bible,* the *Baker Encyclopedia of Psychology,* and the *Evangelical Commentary on the Bible.*

In 1997 when leadership passed to the third generation of Bakers, Dwight Baker felt it was time for the publisher to move beyond a narrowly Reformed perspective. Though Baker had published Wesleyan-Arminian

---

5. Ruark, *House of Zondervan,* 136.

6. Ruark, *House of Zondervan,* 122, and Stan Gundry in personal interview with the author, May 3, 2019.

authors previously, the release in 2000 of Greg Boyd's *God of the Possible*, which supported open theism, touched a nerve with some.

Baker, like Eerdmans, signaled a deliberate move into the Catholic market. In 2009 they began publication of the Catholic Commentary on Sacred Scripture Series, which now has seventeen volumes in print.

All three publishers expanded the number of new titles released per year. IVP's grew to between fifty and sixty in the 2010s. Zondervan produced about fifteen titles a year in the 1980s and has leveled off at about fifty in the last decade. While Baker was producing thirty new titles in the mid-1990s, by 2019 they were releasing seventy.

With these increases came a reduced dependence on European publishers and authors. Standard practices also shifted from importing books from the UK (1940s and 1950s) to licensing (1960s to 2000s) with co-printing thrown into the mix (1990–2010). In the last decade UK and US publishers have mostly stopped licensing and been selling their own books worldwide. As Eerdmans's Jon Pott told me, "Though I did it my whole career, there was not much point in going to the Frankfurt Book Fair in recent years to acquire US rights."[7]

Another common feature was that separate imprints were also established within the larger publishing houses to signal to professors, authors, and booksellers the significance of these efforts. Baker Academic launched in 1999, IVP Academic in 2006, and Zondervan Academic in 2019. Eerdmans didn't feel a need to do so since only a minority of its work was trade publishing, but it did set off Eerdmans Books for Young Readers, which was established in 1995.

NEW AND REVITALIZED PLAYERS

Not only did these four expand, other existing publishers did too. For example, Crossway Books began making significant efforts in academic publishing filling in the gap some felt Baker left when it moved away from its predominantly Reformed publishing program. Like Zondervan, Crossway also used the publication of a Bible translation (the ESV) to springboard into other reference and academic titles.

Kregel Publications, another of the Dutch-heritage publishers in Grand Rapids also known for decades largely as a reprint publisher, established an academic imprint in 2003. While it had previously produced

7. Jon Pott in personal interview with the author, April 30, 2019.

fewer than ten academic titles per year, by 2019 it was releasing about two dozen.

Baylor University Press had been established in 1897 but was revitalized after Carey Newman became director in 2003. They have published across a range of academic disciplines, with an emphasis on the Bible and theology that includes many evangelical and mainline authors.

New academic publishers entered the fray as well. Hendrickson Publishers (1980) grew out of Christian Book Distributors (now Christianbook. com) which was founded by Ray and Stephen Hendrickson.

Advances in technology made other new efforts possible. Wipf and Stock Publishers (1995) began as a joint effort of two West Coast booksellers, John Wipf and Jon Stock. Their unique business model depends on print-on-demand technology rather than stocking books in a warehouse. Without such overhead they have, since the year 2000, been able to produce over 500 new and reprint titles a year, which traditional academic publishing had not found financially supportable.

Lexham Press (2008) is the academic print arm of the otherwise digital efforts of Logos Bible Software.[8] Logos has more than 43,000 titles available electronically from more than 200 publishers.[9] In recent years it has also begun publishing original material for its electronic platform. In 2018 Lexham itself acquired another new academic startup—Weaver Book Company.

Other software companies like Accordance and Olive Tree have also expanded the reach of academic works, providing an important secondary income stream for the original publishers.

The story is not one of unfettered advancement, however. Moody Press deemphasized its academic program. Thomas Nelson began an effort in the 1980s but soon bowed out. Word Books started the high-level Word Biblical Commentary Series but did not follow up with other academic works. The series is now published by Zondervan.

BEHIND THE GROWTH

In the twenty years following the decision to expand IVP's academic publishing, I am sure I thought we were just a very smart, energetic team with the know-how and talent to make things happen. Eventually I began to see

8. In 2014 Logos rebranded the corporation as FaithLife.

9. "Logos Bible Software."

that we were beneficiaries of other forces and developments that made such success possible not only for IVP but for other evangelical publishers. What were some of those?

I've already mentioned one: the availability of quality books from European scholars. One of the less well-known influences behind this was the work of Tyndale House and the Tyndale Fellowship in England. With its origins in the 1930s under the umbrella of Inter-Varsity Fellowship (IVF) in the UK, a group of scholars founded these organizations to promote academic biblical research and publication at the highest levels while supporting evangelicals in their efforts to obtain university posts.[10]

Many books generated by the scholars of Tyndale House and Fellowship beginning in the 1950s were published by IVP-UK and others, which were often picked up for publication by various US publishers. In 1990, Bruce Winter, the warden of Tyndale House, Cambridge, reported, "In the past 10 years the former readers [professors], grantees, and Tyndale House fellows have published 351 books, contributed 271 chapters to books, written 897 articles for learning journals and a large number of dictionary entries."[11] The influence of Tyndale House was worldwide with half the research library's desks in recent decades often being occupied by those from outside the United Kingdom, most from North America.

A second factor which made success possible for IVP and other academic programs was the rise of theological education in the US and Canada. In 1969, for example, the Association of Theological Schools (ATS) collected data from 170 member institutions showing enrollment of 29,815 students. Fifty years later, 276 institutions reported 67,312 enrolled.[12] While the US population had increased 63 percent over this same period, the ATS showed an increase of double that percentage.[13] Clearly, with a usually steady rise in the number of students in classes, more textbooks would be purchased, and more potential authors would be obtaining advanced degrees.

10. See Noll, *Between Faith and Criticism*, 82–85; and Noble, *Tyndale House and Fellowship*.

11. Noble, *Tyndale House and Fellowship*, 237–38.

12. These statistics are drawn from the *Annual Data Tables* and annual *Fact Books on Theological Education* produced by the Association of Theological Schools in the United States and Canada. These numbers represent head count, not full-time equivalents, and include those enrolled in MDiv, Ministerial non-MDiv, General Theological, and Advanced Ministerial programs.

13. US Census Bureau, "US Population by Year."

One arresting example comes from Stan Gundry. When he graduated from Talbot Seminary in 1963, there were seventy-five students. Today more than twelve hundred are enrolled.[14]

A third factor was the influence of Francis Schaeffer and others who validated the life of a Christian mind. Schaeffer, a missionary to Europe's youth in the 1950s and 60s, became an intellectual and cultural guru to the rising generation in North America. His books (fourteen published by IVP alone from 1968 to 1975) sold hundreds of thousands of copies. While not a true scholar himself, the main impression he made was that one could engage secular culture confidently and with intellectual integrity. As a result many pursued academic careers, especially with a vision of integrating a Christian perspective with their fields of study. Barry Hankins highlights several individuals who give direct credit to Schaeffer for their vocational direction including John Walford, William Edgar, Roger Lundin, Jerram Barrs, and Nancy Pearcy.[15]

Other key figures emphasized this message as well. George Marsden, Nicholas Wolterstorff, and Carl F. H. Henry showed how disciplined academic work could be done while modeling Christian intellectual engagement to address cultural movements. Not least, C. S. Lewis did the same in the academic world while also combining a unique winsomeness with intellectual rigor to show the appeal of Christianity to a wider audience.[16]

Finally, two very practical factors were at work. One is that evangelical academic publishers offered lower retail prices than university presses and particularly specialized publishers in Europe like Brill and Peeters. While still priced higher than trade books, quality books at affordable prices were very attractive to professors and students.

The other is the longevity of many academic editors. Stan Gundry at Zondervan and Jon Pott at Eerdmans, for example, each maintained a steady publishing vision at their houses and developed long-term relationships with authors for four decades. Dan Reid and Jim Hoover enjoyed thirty-year tenures at IVP, and I was there for forty. Other publishers gained similar stability and strength from this phenomenon.

---

14. Stan Gundry in personal interview with the author, May 3, 2019; and see Association of Theological Schools in the United States and Canada, "Table 2.15," *Annual Data Tables*.

15. Hankins, *Francis Schaeffer*.

16. Derrick, *Fame of C. S. Lewis*.

CHALLENGES AND HOPES AHEAD

If the story of evangelical academic publishing has largely been one of expansion and rising quality over the last fifty years, what challenges might lie ahead?

The first is not new. Over the last fifty years more evangelicals have obtained degrees from the most prestigious universities, taken positions at these institutions, and published with university presses.[17] Evangelical publishers would very much liked to have published such books but authors have been difficult to persuade. After all, the lure of such highly regarded imprints is hard to ignore. Hard but not impossible. As New Testament scholar Scot McKnight writes, "University presses still have the far greater reputation and far fewer sales!"[18]

The story, however, is not a simple one of publishing competition, of winners and losers. A symbiosis has developed between these two realms. Regarding one discipline, historian Mark Noll comments, "The great contribution of evangelical academic presses to serious, Christian-inflected history-writing since the 1950s has been to give younger scholars an outlet as a way to get going, but then have so-to-speak handed them off to the university press world."[19] Yet such authors are often not lost forever. If a university press contributes to the prestige and platform of an author, their subsequent book with an evangelical publisher might well be of enhanced value.[20]

Second, patterns in higher education are in the midst of substantial disruption. Massive online programs from Grand Canyon and Liberty Universities, for example, have made a few texts into bestsellers. But the huge enrollments have drawn students away from other schools, reducing the use of other texts at those institutions. And when online programs develop their own courses, established publishers are cut out entirely.

The next decades are also likely to see declining enrollment. Rising tuition costs have been one deterrent. In addition, beginning in 2025, enrollments are projected to decline across most of the nation due to a downturn

---

17. Noll, *Between Faith and Criticism*, 122–29; and Ream, Pattengale, and Devers, *The State*, 5–8

18. Scot McKnight in written interview with the author, February 9, 2019. McKnight is professor of New Testament at Northern Seminary in Illinois.

19. Mark Noll in written interview with the author, February 20, 2019.

20. Dan Reid in written interview with the author, February 13, 2019.

in the birth rate following the Great Recession.[21] Publishers will need to be flexible if, for example, theological education moves into the churches (perhaps in partnership with existing institutions).

A third challenge is being victims of our own success. As a result of growth, as an editor put it to me, "We are in a period of academic overpublishing." One publisher told me that previously he could expect to sell about 1,500 copies of a typical academic book in its first two years. Fifteen years later it was down to 300. Several publishers I spoke with reported similar experiences. As a result most are no longer increasing the number of new titles they release each year. One editor said: "We have plenty of knowledge now. Many huge, well-researched, respectable academic books. Today we need more wisdom."

Fourth, publishers will continue to face anti-intellectual pressures from within evangelicalism and anti-evangelical pressures from within the academy. Suspicions about scientists, philosophers, and psychologists are common among conservative believers. Those with fundamentalist impulses continue to react powerfully against scholars whose views vary even modestly from traditional perspectives, seeking to have them dismissed from their institutions or excluded from evangelical societies.

On the other hand, in 2016 the Society of Biblical Literature (SBL) had discussions about possibly banning IVP Academic from exhibiting at its annual conference. The reason was the policy of IVP's parent organization about same-sex relationships.[22] As of this writing, IVP Academic has not been excluded, but the tensions between an institution representing the academy like SBL and a faith-based organization like IVP still remain. Questions are not going away regarding academic freedom and how inclusive the university world will be.

Not only challenges, but opportunities lie ahead. While the situation may be stagnating in North America, Christianity around the world has exploded. Dan Reid writes: "The startling fact is that nearly half of all Christians who have ever lived over the two-thousand-year history of the church are alive today. And the vast majority can read. While North American Christian publishers should resist the impulse to colonize these cultures with Western thinking, surely there are publishing opportunities

---

21. See Grawe, *Demographics*. While there will be a decline, it will not be even across regions or types of institutions, with some even seeing modest gains.

22. See InterVarsity Press, "Joint Statement."

that are awaiting creative and intelligent engagement."[23] This can have two beneficial aspects, by publishers making world voices available in North America as well as around the globe.

A second opportunity is related to the first. Clearly the story of the last fifty years of academic evangelical Christian publishing has largely been white and male—in the makeup of management, editorial employees, and of the author pool. This has closely paralleled the story of evangelicalism in the United States. With uneven steps, and with modestly increasing pace in the last decade, publishing programs like IVP's have begun to more closely reflect the diversity of the church.

I look forward to reading the story of that growth.

BIBLIOGRAPHY

Association of Theological Schools in the United States and Canada. *Annual Data Tables.* https://www.ats.edu/resources/institutional-data/annual-data-tables.
———. *Fact Books on Theological Education.* https://www.ats.edu/resources/institutional-data/annual-data-tables.
———. "Table 2.15: Head Count and Full-Time Equivalent Enrollment by Degree Category, Fall 2018, All Member Schools." In *2018–2019 Annual Data Tables,* www.ats.edu/uploads/resources/institutional-data/annual-data-tables/2018–2019-annual-data-tables.pdf.
Derrick, Stephanie L. *The Fame of C. S. Lewis: A Controversialist's Reception in Britain and America.* Oxford: Oxford University Press, 2018.
Grawe, Nathan D. *Demographics and the Demand for Higher Education.* Baltimore: Johns Hopkins University Press, 2018.
Hankins, Barry. *Francis Schaeffer and the Shaping of Evangelical America.* Grand Rapids: Eerdmans, 2008.
InterVarsity Press. "Joint Statement on IVP Academic & Society of Biblical Literature Matter." November 2016. www.ivpress.com/press-releases/2016/joint-statement-on-ivp-academic-society-of-biblical-literature-sbl-matter.
Le Peau, Andrew T., and Linda Doll. *Heart. Soul. Mind. Strength. An Anecdotal History of InterVarsity Press, 1947–2007.* Downers Grove, IL: InterVarsity, 2006.
"Logos Bible Software." en.wikipedia.org/wiki/Logos_Bible_Software.
Noll, Mark. *Between Faith and Criticism.* Grand Rapids: Baker, 1986, 1991.
Noble, T. A. *Tyndale House and Fellowship: The First Sixty Years.* Leicester, England: InterVarsity, 2006.
Ream, Todd C., Jerry Pattengale, and Christopher J. Devers, eds. *The State of the Evangelical Mind.* Downers Grove, IL: IVP Academic, 2018.
Ruark, James E. *The House of Zondervan.* Grand Rapids: Zondervan, 2006.
Ten Harmsel, Larry, with Reinder Van Till. *An Eerdmans Century 1911–2011.* Grand Rapids: Eerdmans, 2011.

23. Dan Reid in written interview with the author, February 13, 2019.

US Census Bureau. "US Population by Year." https://www.multpl.com/united-states-population/table/by-year.

SANDRA VANDER ZICHT

Thirty Years of Change in Christian Book Publishing

IN THE SIXTIES, WHEN I was growing up, women were generally funneled into one of two careers—nursing or teaching. Since the sight of blood made me queasy, my choice seemed obvious. I would become a high school English teacher.

But during my last semester at Calvin College as a student teacher, I came face to face with a difficult truth. As a high school teacher, you had to be good in academics but you also had to have a martial arts degree in discipline. I didn't and couldn't imagine I ever would attain one.

With a shadow over my career plans, I decided to evade the problem by heading to graduate school and earning an MA in English Language and Literature from the University of Michigan. As I was completing the course, the professor who had encouraged me to pursue an advanced degree suggested I apply for a job as a curriculum editor. After six years in curriculum publishing and five in magazine publishing, Zondervan Publishing House offered me a job as Special Projects Editor in 1985.

I have been and always will be an avid reader. I found my passion: book publishing. During my time at Zondervan, I worked in several different positions in both the marketing and editorial departments. My favorite role was the last and longest—acquiring good books and authors. Over the course of thirty-three years at Zondervan, I saw plenty of changes in the publishing industry. Here are some of the major ones.

CHANGE #1: FROM MANUSCRIPT TO BOOK PROPOSAL

When I first sat in the acquiring chair, authors would mail complete manuscripts for evaluation. I rarely, if ever, needed to read an entire manuscript to determine whether it was a good fit for Zondervan. A few pages, sometimes the first chapter, would be enough for me to make a decision. The job was made far easier by a freelance manuscript submissions editor who screened everything. She forwarded on only the most promising projects. Zondervan would receive more than 3,000 unsolicited manuscripts a year.

Today instead of sending completed manuscripts, authors submit book proposals that are usually accompanied by one to three sample chapters for editors to evaluate. The proposal also summarizes the book, identifies the reader benefit or felt need (the answer to the "What's in it for me?" question), its target audience, and market competition, as well as the author's credentials, platform, and plan for helping the publisher launch the book into the marketplace.

CHANGE #2: FROM UNAGENTED TO AGENTED

While the general publishing world had been doing business with agents for years, only two Christian agents were practicing at the time I began acquiring manuscripts in the late 1980s: Sealy Yates of Yates & Yates Literary Agency and Rick Christian of Alive Communications. Now countless agents serve the Christian marketplace. Even New York agents get a slice of the faith-based publishing pie.

In the early 2000s Zondervan made the decision to stop accepting unsolicited proposals for review. Only those submitted by literary agents would be considered. The one exception was for proposals presented to interested editors at writer's conferences.

Though some in the Christian publishing community jokingly referred to agents as "low-life scum-sucking bottom feeders," most editors would admit that agents provide a useful service, pre-screening potential authors and proposals and helping to find the best projects in the market. One downside in the acquisitions process is that sometimes an unagented author who is already working with an editor will sign with an agent who will then take the author to another publisher. Loyalty is one publishing virtue that's nice to see.

CHANGE #3: SPEED OF COMMUNICATION/ PUBLICATION OR FEDEX AND WANG

In the early days, before FedEx was widespread and computers were available, the pace of publishing was much slower. Manuscripts were edited on paper with red pen and Post-It notes and were mailed to the author, who reviewed the edits by paper, added their own revisions, and then returned them by the US mail. It was not unheard of to take two years or more to publish a book.

In the 1980s Zondervan became one of the first publishers to begin editing on Wang desktop computers. Though these early computers represented an enormous technological advance, editors were required to save their work every half hour or so. Despite these precautions, there were many horror stories of edits being lost and entire manuscripts needing to be re-edited.

With the advent of email, it became possible in the early 1990s to send edited manuscripts back and forth electronically. This opened up the possibility of publishing "instant books"—ones that could be written, edited, and printed in as little as three months. Though the usual publishing timeline was far longer, this new form of communication allowed the company to rush a book into production if market conditions warranted.

CHANGE #4: SIX CHANNELS OF DISTRIBUTION

When I began working at Zondervan, the Christian Bookstore Association (CBA) was our biggest customer by far. In 1992 our sales department was consciously seeking to expand our channels of distribution. Think of the Port Authority of New York/New Jersey. Commuters can choose from many ways to get from the Port Authority to their final destination: a private car, a train, a bus, a taxi, or an Uber. Or they could use their feet on the final leg of their trip. Similarly, there are many ways that a publisher can get books into the hands of interested readers.

I still remember the meeting in 1992 in which VP of Sales Cris Doornbos (currently the president of David C. Cook) unveiled six primary channels of distribution:

- CBA (Christian booksellers)

- ABA (general booksellers, such as Barnes & Noble and Borders)

- General Market/Big Box (retail stores such as Target and Walmart, and wholesale clubs such as Costco and Sam's Club)

- Parachurch (e.g., Focus on the Family)

- E-tailers such as Amazon (1995) and Christian Book Distributors

Expanding these channels of distribution was a way to avoid putting all our eggs in one basket, a strategy that would eventually contribute to the decline of Christian bookstores. At the height of its success, Family Christian Stores had 240 bookstores.

CHANGE #5: DECLINE OF THE CHRISTIAN RETAIL STORE

By the time I retired from Zondervan in the summer of 2018, Amazon had become our biggest customer and the Christian retail store was in sharp decline. In 2015, Family Christian Stores—the largest chain of Christian bookstores—declared Chapter 11 bankruptcy, and in 2017, they closed all of their retail stores. In March 2019, LifeWay Christian Stores (the Southern Baptist equivalent) announced the closing of all of their 170 retail stores.

Prominent author Philip Yancey described the decline of the Christian retail store in the foreword to this book, "Farewell to the Golden Age": "The changes in publishing, especially Christian publishing, stood out sharply to me when I stopped in at the largest annual Christian book convention (International Christian Retail Show, ICRS) in June 2015. At one time 15,000 attended that trade show, a convention so large that only a handful of cities could accommodate it. Now less than 4,000 attend, and in Atlanta it occupied a corner of the huge convention center."

Somewhere along the road CBA changed to ICRS, from the Christian Bookstore Association to the International Christian Retail Show, and Christian bookstores expanded their product from books to other gift items, including Precious Moments figurines, music CDs, T-shirts, and other "Jesus junk"—a term book purists scornfully used to describe the change.

"In the early 1990s," wrote Yancey, "chain stores such as Walmart, Costco, and Sam's Club started picking off bestsellers [such as *Left Behind* and *The Purpose Driven Life*] and general bookstores like Borders (now defunct) and Barnes & Noble greatly expanded their religion departments. Then came Amazon.com, offering deep discounts to siphon off the steady sales that kept small bookstores afloat."

CHANGE #6: MARKETING MOVING FROM PUBLISHER TO AUTHOR

One of the most significant changes in the publishing process has been the shift of marketing from publisher to author. Publishers still mastermind marketing, but the strategy, at least for nonfiction trade books, is for the publisher to support authors' efforts to market their books by way of their platform, particularly their social media platform.

In the early days of my career, authors would hand in their final edits, at which point the marketing department would take over—writing catalog and cover copy, sending out press releases, pitching the book to media, and then scheduling media appearances. Today the author often helps create a launch team before the book is published, preparing the marketplace with tweets, blog posts, and Facebook and Instagram posts. Once the book is released, she sends email blasts to her email distribution list and continues to tweet and post about the book.

Since a large part of the publishing decision is based on platform, publishers look carefully to determine how many blog, Twitter, Instagram, and podcast followers prospective authors have as well as looking at the size of their email distribution list.

Bestselling author Lysa TerKeurst propelled her book *Made to Crave* to number five on the *New York Times* best-seller list in February 2011 with her blog, Twitter, and Instagram posts. She currently has more than 300,000 Twitter followers and nearly 600,000 Instagram followers. In February 2019 Rachel Hollis's second bestselling book *Girl, Stop Apologizing* hit the *New York Times* best-seller list, in large part because of her tireless promotion on social media.

CHANGE #7: THE RISE (AND FALL) OF EBOOKS

I was still at Zondervan to witness the rise of ebooks with the debut of the Kindle in 2007 and the Nook in 2009. Many people predicted the demise of the print book when ebooks became relatively inexpensive and widely available. And ebooks did look like they might replace print books. They could often be purchased for $9.99 and were far more portable than hardcover books.

A decade ago, as the Kindle became easier to use, the sales of ebooks soared, increasing by 400 percent. Then people's love affair with the Kindle cooled, and print book sales started to climb again, fueled in part by the younger generation, who showed a preference for print over digital. Print books become a respite for a generation so engaged digitally.

According to Statista, in 2013, the digital sales market share amounted to just over 12 percent and was expected to more than double by 2018. Although some sources point to a decline in the number of ebooks sold over the past decade, it may be because more and more libraries offer ebooks to their patrons.

CHANGE #8: THE RISE OF AUDIOBOOKS

More recently the sales of audiobooks have surged. In 2018 Zondervan's audio department saw a double-digit rise in sales. Projected sales for audiobooks began to be built into individual project analyses created to determine whether a prospective book might be profitable.

Perhaps the rise of audio has been driven by millennials like my daughter, who gets much of her information by listening to podcasts or audiobooks as she does other things, such as cooking, cleaning, and exercising.

According to research reported in *Publisher's Weekly*, half of all Americans over the age of twelve have listened to an audiobook in the past year. This increase can be attributed to more users listening in cars with in-dash information and entertainment systems. Home listening is the second most popular way of listening to audiobooks.

"Audiobooks are becoming more mainstream, and most of the growth is coming from people using technology to find time in their day to consume more books," said Chris Lynch, president and publisher, Simon & Schuster Audio, to *Forbes* in April 2019.

CHANGE #9: THE RISE OF FEMALE AUTHORS

When I first started in Christian book publishing in 1985, the majority of best-selling authors were male—authors such as Philip Yancey, Gary Smalley, Larry Crabb, and Tim LaHaye. For the most part, authors needed to have a radio program (Dave Ramsey), a TV program (Charles Stanley), or a speaking ministry (Gary Smalley) to help propel their books to best-seller lists.

Then, in the late 1990s and early 2000s, women started writing blogs from their homes. "Whereas motherhood used to mean a very cut-and-dry (and difficult) choice between childrearing and one's career," writes Jill Fehrenbacher, "a new generation of moms are finding that they can have their career cake and eat it too through the power of the weblog."[1]

The rise of women working as bloggers has enabled many to create a new kind of platform from which to launch their books. Publishers took notice and women such as Ann Voskamp, Lysa TerKeurst, Glennon Melton Doyle, and Heather Armstrong became best-selling authors.

WHAT HASN'T CHANGED

Though many things have changed in the publishing of books, some things remain the same.

What book editors/publishers are looking for hasn't changed, although they may use a different terminology to describe it today. What editors are looking for can be sorted into the three Cs: concept, craft, and crowd.

A concept is the idea of the book, what the book is about. In the early 1990s, when I met psychologists Henry Cloud and John Townsend, they had a roster of books they wanted to publish, but one idea stood head and shoulders above the rest: boundaries. *Boundaries* was actually the second book in the publishing plan that they and their agent presented to us, but the entire team knew that it was the best idea with which to begin our publishing relationship.

A great concept is always enhanced by the right title and subtitle. When *Boundaries* was announced in the 1992 Zondervan catalog, the subtitle was "Gaining Control of Your Life." We ended up changing the subtitle to "When to Say Yes, When to Say No, To Take Control of Your Life." To date, *Boundaries* has sold more than two million copies.

Second to a great concept is craft, by which I simply mean great writing. One best-selling author that Zondervan signed simply for her exquisite writing was Ann Voskamp. The publishing committee fell in love with her writing and decided to sign her, even though the idea—gratitude—wasn't all that new and her platform didn't appear to be large. Again title (and packaging) played a part in presenting her to the world. The original title,

1. Fehrenbacher, "Rise."

God in the Moment, was changed to *One Thousand Gifts*, which more accurately captured the unique angle of the book. Voskamp's book went on to sell a million copies in the first year.

Crowd—the third C—is simply the potential author's tribe. Who will help the author get the word out about her book? Today it's helpful for an author to have a huge following on Facebook, Instagram, or Twitter, but even more effective is a large email distribution list that a publisher can use to market the book. This C is often labeled as an author's *platform*. Despite the importance of social media today, platform has always been important when it comes to publishing trade books.

Book editors are always searching for authors who have something new to say and who can say it well. They are on the hunt for books that will move readers to tears or laughter or tell them something fascinating or important that they don't already know. A passionate editor can often convince a publisher to take a chance on a new author who may not yet have a strong platform.

Though editing has been downplayed in recent years, good editing can help a book find its audience. A well-edited book will start word of mouth—which is something that all best-selling books have in common. If you love a book you've just read, you will tell your circle of family and friends and they will in turn tell others.

Though editing software programs like Grammarly promise even the editing of "style," no editing programs rival the human brain God has made, which can create, adjust, adapt, fix, and even write copy for the author whose work is wisely put in the hands of an editor. Maxwell Perkins, the protagonist of A. Scott Berg's book *Editor of Genius*, edited Ernest Hemingway, F. Scott Fitzgerald, and Thomas Wolfe. Grammarly couldn't edit them back then, and Hemingway, Fitzgerald, and Wolfe wouldn't let it happen today.

Behind every published book is an editor who believed in its author or its idea, an editor who was willing to fight for what she loved and was willing to make it the best it could be. One author I fell in love with when I heard her story of adopting two boys from Africa was Lysa TerKeurst. The book idea I fell in love with was *Made to Crave*. I saw an idea that women would resonate with: satisfying one's deepest desires with God, not food. The publishing committee initially saw the book as just another diet book, but we convinced them that it was more than that. The book went on to hit the *New York Times* best-seller list.

So many changes in Christian book publishing have not dimmed my love of the industry. Good and bad books and everything in between will continue to be published. Bad books show us what good books look like. Good books bring us to laughter and tears and maybe a few deep thoughts. And the best books will tell us something that we don't already know (maybe, about God and ourselves).

BIBLIOGRAPHY

Fehrenbacher, Jill. "The Rise of the Mom Blogger." https://www.americanexpress.com/en-us/business/trends-and-insights/articles/the-rise-of-the-mom-blogger-1/.

JON POTT

In Two Worlds

WHEN I WALKED THROUGH the door at Eerdmans in the late spring of 1968, needing a job to get through "just one more year" of hiatus from grad school, religious publishing was not in my plan for life. Certainly not at Eerdmans. Wasn't this the company responsible for publishing all those ultraconservative Reformed scholastics we as Calvin College students had wanted to get as far behind us as possible? And what about those cringe-making Sugar Creek Gang books out of my youth, Big Jim piously counseling Little Jim behind the shed? Still, Eerdmans was also, I knew, the publisher of Henry Zylstra's *Testament of Vision,* a little volume of essays that for many of us students at Calvin had been a lodestar to the meaning of a Christian liberal education. And, for all the theological rigidity of a Louis Berkhof and his ilk, there was also the relative expansiveness of, say, Herman Bavinck or Abraham Kuyper, not to mention Calvin himself. But trumping everything for me at the moment was that I had friends already at the company who seemed to feel that the ship was setting sail now to some heady fresh winds.

The Eerdmans I joined that June was, in fact, alive with political and social protest. These were the days of the Vietnam War, into which one of its editors had been dragged (creating a vacancy for me); of the war on poverty, the war for which we did applaud the beleaguered Lyndon Johnson; and of the civil rights movement, in which a member of our marketing department had marched from Selma. We had published, or would soon publish, the likes of *The Vietnam War: Christian Perspectives* (1967); *Uncertain Resurrection: The Poor People's Washington Campaign* (1969); and *Black Reflections on White Power* (1969). In 1962, the same year in which he famously got public attention from Karl Barth touring America, lawyer William Stringfellow published with Eerdmans his activist tract *A Private and Public Faith*. And in 1969 came Arthur Gish's *The New Left and Christian Radicalism*, a summons to the social radicalism of the "left wing" of the Reformation. That summons out of the Anabaptist tradition soon took on magisterial theological form in John Howard Yoder's *The Politics of Jesus* (1972), one of those landscape-changing classics that seem to appear less often now. The Yoder legacy has, over the years, lived on in the work of others as well, nowhere more importantly than in the work of Stanley Hauerwas, a powerful ongoing presence in his own right and an influence beyond through his many students.

Eventually, in 1984 and from a very different quarter—first Lutheran, then Catholic—came Richard John Neuhaus and his *Naked Public Square*, with its call for public Christian engagement in the context of American secularism, another landmark book in the Eerdmans program that entered the religious vocabulary and became a rallying cry for so-called neoconservatism.

At Eerdmans, no matter what other past associations, this urge to social and cultural activism was fed by an important theological stream of its own, beginning in Calvinism itself and its emphasis on creation and the sovereignty of God, but, for many in the Dutch-Calvinist community, welling with special force in that late-nineteenth-century Dutch pastor, theologian, journalist, public intellectual, and political force who was Abraham Kuyper (1837–1920). Kuyper became briefly prime minister of the Netherlands and was one of the founders of the Free University of Amsterdam. Many of his adherents immigrated to the US and helped to shape the theological ethos of the Dutch-Calvinist community out of which Eerdmans came and in which a number of us grew up and were educated. He himself came over in 1898 to deliver the Stone Lectures at Princeton Seminary, which were ultimately published by Eerdmans in 1931 as *Lectures on Calvinism* and are still iconically in print. These lectures became an underlying manifesto in that part of the Dutch-Calvinist academic world that formed many of us, a ringing summons to open inquiry and a transformative Christian engagement with all spheres of life. Not only the goodness of the original creation, but also the goodness of human culture and of human institutions, as wrought by God's ongoing "common grace," was to be gratefully affirmed; and what had been corrupted by sin—Calvinists are not known to soft-pedal sin—was not to be avoided but knowledgeably addressed and transformed in the kingdom enterprise. Whatever the promises of eternity, there was important work to be done in the here and now. And no talk, please, of anything "spiritual," of what is "sacred" rather than "secular." There is not, Kuyper famously pronounced, "one thumb's width" over which Christ is not Lord!

Books by Kuyper, about Kuyper, and in the tradition of Kuyper were an ongoing presence in the Eerdmans program I knew. This was so very explicitly in, for example, the political and social scholarship of Richard Mouw (*Political Evangelism*, 1973, etc.), who took his Kuyperianism from Calvin College to the wider evangelical stage of Fuller Seminary, as had Lewis Smedes some years before. And It was also so in the broad contribution of philosopher Nicholas Wolterstorff, who, in the Kuyper Lectures of 1981, given at Kuyper's Free University and published by Eerdmans as *Until Justice and Peace Embrace* (1983), laid out the paradigm distinction between approaches to culture that are escapist and protectionist, "avertive," as he put it—a critique of both the evangelical world and the world of Reformed pietism—and those that mean to be culturally engaged and "transformative." His own highly transformative approach was brought to bear in books for Eerdmans and other publishers on a broad range of subjects from peace and justice to worship and liturgy, and from the arts to Christian education, not to mention his specialist work in the philosophy of religion itself, in particular, in epistemology.

It is this spirit of open and transformative inquiry, then, that, however unnecessary it might have seemed to state (the company never in my time had a formal mission statement), animated a number of us at Eerdmans over the years. Not that the Kuyperian voice was the only voice in the choir, as more members ecumenically joined the staff, bringing their own perspectives— Methodist, Mennonite, Episcopal, Baptist, Catholic, and a few not religious at all. But it was surely the voice of my two splendid predecessors as editor-in-chief, Calvin Bulthuis and Marlin VanElderin. And all of us, no matter what our particular blend of religious tradition and irreverent iconoclasm, were energized by a commitment to intellectual engagement and cultural action. And all of this idealism was now in the energetic hands of Bill Eerdmans, Jr., who had taken over the company presidency from his father in 1965 and had his own inspiriting vision for doing the needed good. Doing the needed good meant that "any day was a good day to publish a good book," tacking to market winds as needed, but never allowing these winds to blow the ship off course.

The good we tried to do was pretty much for an audience of academics, pastors, and well-educated laity. No inspirational material. No celebrity effusions. No popular self-help, though we were intensely proud of reflective Christian-life books like those by Eugene Peterson. And, in good Kuyperean fashion, the subjects we covered—sometimes controversially—ranged widely, well beyond the core religious disciplines of theology and biblical studies to ethics and social issues, to the philosophy of religion, to history, and to the arts—especially literature, but also music, film, and the visual arts.

In my early days in the editorial department, the program was already attracting the attention some of the most creative minds emerging onto a larger academic stage from our own Calvin College and its sister institutions. These included Smedes, Wolterstorff, and Mouw, but also, over time, the likes of George Marsden, Ronald Wells, Mary Stewart Van Leeuwen, Allen Verhey, and Cornelius Plantinga, Jr. When these energetic minds, and others in the Dutch-Reformed community, weren't publishing in the book program itself, they were a vibrant presence in *The Reformed Journal*, which Eerdmans published ten times a year for nearly forty years. This magazine, with an authorship and audience that grew well beyond its native soil, had a wonderfully symbiotic relationship with the book program, cultivating the same network and enlarging it.

By the early seventies, what was coming out of the Dutch-Calvinist academic community was beginning to make common cause with the scholarly renaissance taking hold in the evangelical world, notably, for us, at Wheaton College and Fuller Seminary, but elsewhere as well. Whatever our own past publishing involvement with American fundamentalism—which we tried to see, perhaps a little too conveniently, as an amusing anomaly, not who we really were—figures like E. J. Carnell at Fuller and the broadly influential Carl F. H. Henry were also importantly in the background. In fact, Carl Henry's *The Uneasy Conscience of Modern Fundamentalism* had appeared in 1947, boldly summoning evangelicals to bring the fundamentals of the faith to bear on contemporary culture in ways that were again relevant and academically credible. At Wheaton, the torch for renewal was carried by, among others, philosopher Arthur Holmes, whose *Faith Seeks Understanding* (1971) and *The Idea of a Christian College* (1974) became classics for Eerdmans, and by literary scholar Clyde Kilby, who was instrumental in our ongoing publication of books by and about C. S. Lewis and his circle.

From figures like these the torch was passed to students like Mark Noll, C. Stephen Evans, Roger Lundin, and Marianne Meye Thompson, all of whom attended Wheaton and became part of our exponentially growing brain trust. It was historian Mark Noll who, picking up in a new day the Carl Henry summons to cultural engagement, published with Eerdmans in 1994 *The Scandal of the Evangelical Mind,* the opening sentence of which lamented that there hadn't, in recent decades, been much of a mind.

But whatever Eerdmans' role in encouraging the growing coalition between progressive Dutch-Calvinist and progressive evangelical thinkers, the company had also, in a time when denominational identity and corresponding loyalty to denominational publishing houses was breaking down, become increasingly attractive to many mainline Protestant and Catholic scholars concerned to recover a classic Christianity they thought had all too often thinned to the vanishing point in their respective traditions. The Eerdmans program had repudiated fundamentalism, but it certainly meant to assert with vigor the claims of historic Christianity. Not that it didn't require image-building to convince mainline scholars that, whatever the fundamentalist incursions of the past, we were essentially Reformed mainliners, and whatever the Calvinist scholasticism that was more definitively a part of our tradition, this, too, was not a history that fully defined us and certainly did not define us now. We also had on the list more open older Dutch theologians like Kuyper and Bavinck and, in recent years, G. C. Berkhouwer and Hendrikus Berkhof. Behind all this, of course, lay translations of Calvin himself, and, theologically further back yet, our widely known sets of the church fathers, dated, but a convenient—perhaps in some cases only—source for the patristics in English.

All this was now being importantly augmented by the company's virtual subprogram in books by and about Karl Barth, out of which came, eventually, the systematics of one of Barth's most prominent pupils, Wolfhart Pannenberg. And taking their place alongside these figures, from various traditions, were influential mainline theologians and other scholars like Martin Marty, David Noel Freedman, Paul Achtemeier, James D. G. Dunn, Daniel Migliori, Gilbert Meilaender, Wentzel van Huysteen, Max Stackhouse, Don Browning, and the feisty Lutheran tandem-duo of Carl Braaten and Robert Jenson—all these joined by a growing number of younger academics.

Such theologians—and scholars across the disciplines, both Protestant and Catholic—were increasingly in conversation with evangelical crossover figures like British theologians Colin Gunton, Oliver O'Donovan, and Anthony Thiselton. Other disciplines included history, where an Edwin Gaustad could be in the same catalog with Mark Noll and George Marsden, and also the philosophy of religion, where the growing diverse guild of Christian philosophers, energized not least by Dutch-Calvinist philosophers Nicholas Wolterstorff and Alvin Plantinga, found Eerdmans a helpful vehicle to convey their work to a nonspecialist readership.

Reputation built upon reputation, not least in biblical studies, economically the most important area in the program, with the fall convention of the Society of Biblical Literature, combined with that of the American Academy of Religion (the AAR/SBL), being its central venue. Historically, the Eerdmans biblical-studies tradition could boast, along with other prominent reference works, the famed Kittel-Friedrich *Theological Dictionary of the New Testament*. This monumental work was translated for us by the indefatigable Geoffrey Bromiley of Fuller Seminary, who also translated much Barth for us and later served as both translator and editor of *The Encyclopedia of Christianity*, an altogether mainline German project we took on in part precisely to enhance our mainline image. These major reference works played across the spectrum of broadly respected scholarship and, over the years, were joined by such works as *Eerdmans Dictionary of the Bible*, *Eerdmans Commentary on the Bible*, and *The Eerdmans Dictionary of Early Judaism*, all of them bearing a distinguished mainline or Catholic provenance. Such books took their place beside the reference works and monographs being produced on the evangelical side, these owing much to the pioneering work of F. F. Bruce and continuing in the work of I. Howard Marshall, Gordon Fee, Robert Hubbard, Joel Green, Marianne Meye Thompson, and many others. In the Eerdmans textbook *Introducing the New Testament: Its Literature and Theology*, authors Green and Meye Thompson were joined by esteemed mainline scholar Paul J. Achtemeier.

And so it went, as Eerdmans built and nurtured its mainline and Catholic reputation while simultaneously nurturing its relationship to congenial evangelical scholarship as the two came more and more into dialogue in the academy and the church. The lines were, in fact, often becoming blurred, and our attempt was to cultivate the growing common ground.

It will be apparent even from the brief survey above that, as befits our Dutch pedigree, the company has also over the years been a bridge to European publishers and their authors. In a late-life interview, William B. Eerdmans, Sr., mentions Kok Publishing in the Netherlands as a model for his own venture in America, and we retained close ties to them throughout much of my time, adding other Dutch publishers as well. Eerdmans, Sr., had himself made many trips to the Netherlands, but also to the UK, forging relationships that endure today and have considerably widened. Eerdmans, far longer than the American evangelical publishers, has been a fixture at the Frankfurt Book Fair, the main venue for international rights exchanges and the centerpiece of year-long contact. Increasingly, as scholarship itself has internationalized, the contact has extended directly to authors themselves.

A final bridge. Given the company's deep aversion to distinguishing sacred and secular—one reason why, we might note, it has avoided a program in "Christian fiction"—it will be no surprise that the general market, including the nonreligious market, has been of abiding interest. Along with an award-winning children's imprint that is not explicitly religious at all, the adult program has long published nonreligious history and biography, especially regional, never losing sight of its own ethnic roots.

But besides publishing nonreligious books for the general trade, the company has also, of course, been keenly concerned to reach the general market with relevant religious books. Reaching this market could, however, be frustrating, given the rigid compartmentalizing of religion in most general trade stores. Any book by a religious publisher almost automatically went into the religion section, even if it dealt with a widely discussed public issue like abortion and in a way that would seem to qualify it for display among books on, say, politics and society, where it might have been noticed by a readership not inclined to venture into religion as such. The Neuhaus "naked public square" extended all too often into the bookstore itself, a ghettoizing of religion that has now, however regrettable the decline of the bookstore, been mitigated to some extent by online marketing.

The story of Eerdmans in my time, then, is the story of a company driven by an impulse for cultural transformation arising, in good part, out of its Dutch-Calvinist tradition and a company that, given its particular history, found itself engaged with two worlds coming together in a seismic shift in the religious intellectual landscape. This shift created a significant new area of overlapping interests and common cause. By virtue of its evangelical history, but also by virtue of its even deeper mainline Reformed heritage, the company could appeal credibly to both sides as they pursued their own ends but also connected. Fuller Seminary and Duke Divinity School could be equally home to the Eerdmans program—not to mention

Princeton Seminary, with which Eerdmans has had a long and rich past. The company's intellectual commodiousness has furthermore allowed it to publish ecumenically, and its roots in Europe have encouraged it to publish internationally.

In pursuing its mission, Eerdmans has been greatly helped by its independence as a family-owned business, an independence resolutely protected by its owners and buoyed historically by a strong backlist (harder, it would seem, to build and sustain in today's more fluid, less stable publishing world) and by an openness to exploring creative options to support even highly specialized academic projects. As a company not beholden to the policies of any umbrella organization or institution, it has had wide latitude in the views it can publish, and as family-owned business, it also has not been subject to stockholders for whom its publishing aims might be compromised.

But whatever its corporate independence, the company has never seen itself as freestanding in its cause. This commitment, in a period during which author-publisher loyalties were generally breaking down, was often reciprocated by gratifying loyalty from its network of authors. The company's publishing aim has first of all been to serve the intellectual needs of the church, an educated laity, and the religious academy. Education, to judge by that late-life interview with its founder, is altogether how it saw its calling from the start: "We are not missionaries, we Hollanders," the elder Eerdmans said (we must forgive him a little excess). "We are not missionaries. We are not evangelists. We are educators, and I think that is the gift the Lord has given us."

ROY M. CARLISLE

Paradigmatic Shifts in Christian Publishing: An Editorial Perspective on the Last Fifty Years (1969–2020)

FOR MOST OF THE twentieth century, the large majority of Christian books were published by distinct religious publishers located all over the US. Although religious book divisions in New York at Doubleday, Macmillan, and Harper & Row (later HarperCollins) existed, that was the extent of religious publishing by the large secular publishing houses. That model has changed. Harper still has a religious book division in San Francisco, but the religious divisions in the other major New York publishing houses have disappeared. For a number of reasons, including recognition of how lucrative the Christian market was, the big New York houses purchased individual Christian publishers and set them up to function as wholly owned subsidiaries or they set up imprints within the corporate structure. For example, Harper-Collins has a Christian Publishing Group division that includes HarperOne (formerly HarperSanFrancisco), Zondervan, Thomas Nelson, W Publishing, plus other smaller entities. Simon & Schuster's Christian division was Howard Books. The Hachette Book Group purchased and merged Worthy Publishing and FaithWords, two Christian imprints, into Hachette Nashville. Penguin Random House has a Christian imprint, WaterBrook & Multnomah, located under its Crown imprint.

All these subsidiaries, imprints, or divisions have had ups and downs financially but most have been successful. Generally the sales figures for Christian books published by these corporations prove that Christian book publishing is good business in the US. The American Association of

Publishers reports 6.9 percent growth by religious presses from 2015–2016 to $1.13 billion. And from 2017 to 2018 the increase in revenue was 8.1 percent.[1]

Many of these ownership changes, and the financial success that followed for some, grew out of subtle and not-so-subtle shifts within the Christian community itself. In particular, Christian publishing faced three paradigmatic shifts: a new emphasis on personal narratives, a new permeability in the boundaries of denominations and other religious affiliations, and a new emphasis on the inner life. Let's take a closer look at each of these shifts and their implications for and manifestation in Christian publishing.

SHIFT #1: BIBLICAL NARRATIVES VS. PERSONAL NARRATIVES

In the early 1970s, I was general manager of an expanding religious bookstore at Fuller Theological Seminary in downtown Pasadena, California. When the bookstore moved one block off campus, both staff and inventory grew rather quickly. Paperback popular Christian titles aimed at general readers were among the titles we stocked. Until then, neither I nor my staff had read popular Christian books. As graduate theological students, we read and studied academic texts for our classes. So, in order to know what to buy and stock in the store, we were forced to learn about popular Christian books. Most were published by Christian publishers such as Zondervan, Tyndale, Baker, Nelson, Revell, Harvest House, InterVarsity, Moody, Bethany, Gospel Light, Word, Crossway, and a few mainline Christian publishers such as Abingdon, John Knox, Westminster, Herald Press, Broadman, Holman, Fortress, Concordia, and Gospel Publishing.

I soon discovered that popular Christian books had not quite caught up with the times. In the aftermath of the 1960s countercultural dynamics and the advent of "the pill,"[2] which facilitated a sexual revolution already underway, I noticed that these books lacked expressions of honest feelings, discussions of topics like sex or drugs, and truthful explorations of ecstatic emotional states and doubts or questions about faith.

The best-selling books of those times, titles such as *The Late Great Planet Earth*, *The Battle for the Bible*, and *Move Ahead with Possibility*

1. Danziger, "Despite Lifeway Closing."
2. Eig, *Birth of the Pill*, 299.

Thinking,[3] were generally based on a biblical idea, principle, or passage, but the authors never talked about thoughts or feelings such as doubts and fears. And the narrative never said there was more than one way to understand the biblical text. These kinds of "biblical narratives" were never written from the point of view of real people with difficult feelings and troubling thoughts. The only exceptions were books about the charismatic movement. For example, a book published in 1970, *Nine O'Clock in the Morning* by Dennis Bennett, an Episcopal priest, told of his "baptism in the Holy Spirit and speaking in tongues." It became a huge bestseller and is now considered a classic text and it was one of the books that initiated the charismatic movement in the 1970s. Bennett's book and other charismatic books were very different because they focused on new feelings and experiences. Most Christian publishers, however, were skeptical of the legitimacy of the charismatic movement. So, many of those books were published by new start-up Christian houses. These "charismatic" books were almost completely about complex human desires and feelings and individual reactions to alleged supernatural events. In contrast, most other Christian books seldom, if ever, delved into these areas, at least partially because this would have required authors to honestly express their own feelings, which was not the standard in Christian publishing.

Popular Christian titles, however, did sell well, even in our seminary store, and our bookstore team wondered whether laypeople preferred reading books with no emotional expressions. Or did they only want to read books about so-called "biblical" topics and spiritual principles?

Then two other books precipitated a seismic shift from impersonal narratives based on biblical themes to explorations of personal experience enlightened by faith: In *A Taste of New Wine*, J. Keith Miller[4] shared his personal struggle with doubts, fears, and addictions, and *The Total Woman* by Marable Morgan[5] talked about sex, sensuality, and relationship issues. Both books sold millions of copies, alerting Christian publishers to a significant shift in what customers wanted.

At the time, Christian publishers and Christian retailers wrestled with these "honest" Christian books—and that wrestling has continued for decades. Even today, many Christian bookstores are hesitant to stock

3. Lindsey, with Carlson, *Late Great Planet Earth*; Lindsell, *Battle for the Bible*; Schuller, *Move Ahead*.

4. Miller, *Taste of New Wine*.

5. Morgan, *Total Woman*.

books with personal topics such as sexuality. For example, in 2012, Rachel Held Evans, the late journalist and Christian writer, published *A Year of Biblical Womanhood: How a Liberated Woman Found Herself Sitting on Her Roof, Covering Her Head, and Calling Her Husband Master.*[6] Her publisher, Thomas Nelson, informed her that the LifeWay Bookstore chain would not stock the book because she used the word *vagina* twice.[7]

Contemporary examples of these more honest books include the *New York Times* bestseller *Blue Like Jazz* by Donald Miller and the best-selling *Traveling Mercies* by Anne Lamott. She says, "I try to write the books I would love to come upon, that are honest, concerned with real lives, human hearts, spiritual transformation, families, secrets, wonder, craziness—and that can make me laugh."[8]

Clearly, this new era of emotional, theological, and intellectual transparency that began to gain traction in the late 1970s was not predicted by anyone in Christian publishing.

As part of this shift, pressure from the marketplace, with best-selling authors like J. Keith Miller, Anne Lamott, Donald Miller, Kathleen Norris, Chuck Colson, Richard J. Foster, and Paula D'Arcy forced publishers and bookstores to stop their implicit emotional censorship that had long pervaded the conservative evangelical Christian publishing world, and publish more honest, almost confessional, narratives. This resulted in Christian books crossing over into markets that were not solely Christian-based, and many more people were exposed to honest storytelling with a Christian subplot. This was one of the more profound shifts in Christian publishing during the last century. It was aided and abetted by a new openness as many Christians moved across boundaries between denominations and other insular groups, as we see in shift #2.

SHIFT #2: MOVEMENTS IN AFFILIATIONS

I have a 1980 picture of Jim Wallis, the founder of Sojourners and a *New York Times* best-selling author, standing on a balcony of a hotel in Daytona Beach, Florida. The El Caribe Resort and Conference Center was owned by a friend of his. She had invited us to work on Jim's new book, published

6. Evans, *Year of Biblical Womanhood.*
7. *Guardian*, "Mention of Vagina."
8. Lamott, Brainyquote.

as *The Call to Conversion*,[9] at the hotel as a way to both focus our attention and give us a break from our normally busy schedules. Jim has always known which book he wants to write next, but on this and other occasions he invited my editorial input on the structure and topic of his text. We met at the El Caribe more than once, but on this particular work holiday, our conversations made it clear to me that there was a synthesis of "markets" for Jim's books: his ministry and mission were aimed at people in the church who cared about social justice, politics, culture, and faith. Those potential readers could be evangelicals, Catholics, mainline denominational members, and parachurch ministry staff.

I then realized that this same "market" dynamic had been true of the Christian charismatic movement back in the early 1970s. At that time, I had had my own charismatic experience. I was a member of the Presbyterian Church, but I attended a Foursquare Church in Van Nuys, California. My charismatic friends at seminary attended different religious communities and churches. Our friendships were based on our common experiences and not on our religious affiliations. As a bookstore manager in the seventies, these affiliations hadn't struck me as important or unusual. Now, as an editor and publisher in the eighties, I realized this might mean something new and profound was emerging in the religious landscape of American Christians. If that were true, it could subsequently affect Christian publishing in a significant way. What were the ramifications when two charismatics from different denominations or two social justice advocates or two feminists from completely different groups "felt" closer to each other than they did to members of their own official denominations or groups?

How did this come about? It may be that this phenomenon was at least partially rooted in the cultural upheaval of the 1960s. People who had come of age during that time took the questioning of authority as a given. As a result, they began to move across boundaries of race, political orientation, gender, and religion. Now these attitudes were being manifested in new ways, allowing new affiliations that affirmed the reality of life experience, including the experience of faith. Younger people, especially, began to claim a new kind of inner authority, and were drawn to others with similar experiences.

Simply stated, this shift in affiliation revealed that some, and perhaps even many, Christians felt more connected to people in transdenominational groups than they did to people in their own denominations. A corollary

9. Wallis, *Call to Conversion*.

to this shift was that denominational publishing would, of necessity, need to change significantly. Many denominational publishers realized that they had to move with this shift, or they would likely lose their markets. In the past, those markets had been fairly stable. If I wanted to reach Lutherans, I would find a well-known Lutheran author to write a book and publish that book with a Lutheran publisher. But as the "ground of affiliations" shifted, publishers had to find authors who could speak to people of all denominations. Although these shifts in Christian publishing were not acknowledged consciously or even written about in periodicals, I had made mental notes and began looking for other shifts that might be important in this very diverse world of religious and Christian publishing.

This paradigmatic shift of affiliations may have acted as a kind of bridge between the shift from honest personal narratives toward development of the inner spiritual life. As people learned to honor their own inner authority and experience, which allowed them to move more fluidly among denominations and other traditional groups, this paradigmatic shift prepared the way for the next: the movement from an emphasis on "correct" Christian behavior to the development of the inner life, in which one takes on a new kind of personal responsibility for one's journey of faith rather than adhering to the guidelines and strictures of a denominational or dogmatic approach to faith.

SHIFT #3: CHRISTIAN BEHAVIOR VS. THE INNER LIFE

When I made a profession of Christian faith in the spring of 1966 during my freshman year at Whitman College in Walla Walla, Washington, I sensed changes within my conscious understanding of the world and noticed shifts in my own inner life. But what I soon discovered was that others judged my faith by my behavior. While I do agree that behavior is a factor in determining whether someone has embraced a Christian approach to living, I believe behavior should never be the sole factor in that judgment. Believers are all at different points on the path toward God, so behavior is often an inaccurate indicator of the state of someone's soul. But if behavior is the only criterion for faithful living, then sexual feelings, smoking, drinking, or dancing might indicate a rather immature and very poor example of a "being" Christian. And this "behavioristic" judgment comes both from people who agreed with the profound truth of the Christian story as well as those who didn't. I and others felt like it was not quite the correct criteria for judging Christian maturity.

Personally I was grateful that by entering the world of faith, my heart, soul, and mind had been opened to the reality of a spiritual world that I did not know existed before those early morning moments on May 5, 1966. In seminary I slowly began to understand that the Christian life was much richer and more nuanced than trying to maintain perfect "Christian" behavior. But even during those life-changing years in seminary, many of us still only superficially understood the dynamics of the inner life, particularly the movement from doing to being. At that point, I couldn't have imagined how profound the shift from doing to being would be in my own life, much less how this shift would eventually manifest itself in the publishing industry. This new focus on the inner life meant that prayer, meditation, contemplation, and other spiritual practices were becoming more and more important, which paralleled a similar movement within the larger American church community. Again, adherents were moving beyond denominational lines.

These spiritual practices that helped grow one's soul blossomed fully during the late 1970s and eighties. The movement toward experiencing an inner-directed spiritual life was accompanied by a strong and clear movement away from having to believe the "right" ideas or biblical propositions. My professional life also emphasized this shift because I published a book in 1978 entitled *Celebration of Discipline: The Path to Spiritual Growth* by Richard J. Foster.[10] Although it took a while for that book to gain sales traction, it—almost like no other book of its time—eventually became a huge bestseller and sparked a movement toward deeper spiritual practice. What startled everyone was that it sold to Catholics, conservative evangelicals, and mainline Christians. Here was a Quaker writer trained in a Reformed theological seminary who was metabolizing Catholic spiritual disciplines and Quaker devotional materials into language that appealed to all people of faith. This was a phenomenon. But today even classically evangelical publishing houses like InterVarsity Press (IVP) have imprints for books on spirituality and spiritual formation (IVP has Formatio). No religious book publisher today could even imagine not publishing books on deeper

10. In 1978 at Harper we published one of the first books I had acquired and edited: Foster's *Celebration of Discipline*. It was one of the many important titles that helped make the shift from doing to being. It was a book about the classic spiritual disciplines written in a way that even evangelicals could embrace its teachings: with its emphasis on training (for a change in your inner life) vs. trying (to behave in a way that was "perfect.")

131

spirituality for any believer, so this shift has crossed all lines—denominational, theological, and phenomenological.

CONCLUSION

These three shifts—(1) from biblical narratives to personal narratives, (2) from niche denominational interests and affiliations to transdenominational connections (shifts in affiliations), and (3) from an emphasis on behavior to a focus on inner life (doing to being)—together represent crucial and profound changes that have taken place in the Christian publishing industry in the last five decades. In 1969, people in Christian publishing would have been hard-pressed to envision what would come into being and the resulting transformation of both the Christian community and publishing industry. Our reflection on the past should also cause us to reflect on the future. Perhaps what we can celebrate is the resilience and vision of the Christian publishing industry over the last fifty years and how—though not always smoothly or easily—it adapted both to market realities and the reality of the movement of the Spirit in the lives of people of faith. Clearly that means the Spirit also moves in Christian (and even secular) publishing houses!

RELEVANT READING

1. *Shift 1*: The authors I recommend reading to help you discover this shift to personal storytelling include the following: Sue Monk Kidd's *Dance of the Dissident Daughter*, Annie Lamott's *Traveling Mercies*, Bruce Larson's *The One and Only You*, Don Miller's *Blue Like Jazz*, J. Keith Miller's *The Taste of New Wine*, and Lewis B. Smedes's *Forgive and Forget*.

2. *Shift 2*: The authors I recommend reading to help you discover this affiliation shift include the following: Carmen Renee Berry's *When Helping You is Hurting Me*, Dennis Bennett's *Nine O'Clock in the Morning*, Paula D'Arcy's *Gift of the Red Bird*, Richard Quebedeaux's *The New Charismatics*, and Jim Wallis's *The Soul of Politics*.

3. *Shift 3*: The authors I recommend reading to help you discover this shift include the following: Carmen Renee Berry's *Is Your Body Trying*

to Tell You Something?, Tilden Edwards's *Spiritual Friend*, Richard J. Foster's *Celebration of Discipline*, Dallas Willard's *The Divine Conspiracy*, and Fr. Richard. Rohr's *Everything Belongs*.

BIBLIOGRAPHY

Danziger, Pamela N. "Despite Lifeway Closing 170 Bookstores, Christian Bookselling Will Rise Again." *Forbes*, April 17, 2019. https://www.forbes.com/sites/pamdanziger /2019/04/17/despite-lifeway-closing-170-bookstores-christian-bookselling-will-rise-again/#80470f7f219b.

Eig, Jonathan. *The Birth of the Pill: How Four Crusaders Reinvented Sex and Launched a Revolution*. New York: W. W. Norton, 2014.

Evans, Rachel Held. *A Year of Biblical Womanhood: How a Liberated Woman Found Herself Sitting on Her Roof, Covering Her Head, and Calling Her Husband Master*. Nashville: Thomas Nelson, 2012.

Foster, Richard J. *Celebration of Discipline: The Path to Spiritual Growth*. San Franciso: HarperSanFrancisco, 1978.

The Guardian. "Mention of Vagina Causes Evangelical Bookshop to Refuse Book, Claims Author." October 17, 2021. https://www.theguardian.com/books/2012/oct/17/ mention-vagina-evangelical-bookshop.

Lamott, Anne. Brainyquote. https://www.brainyquote.com/quotes/anne_lamott_573876.

Lindsell, Harold. *The Battle for the Bible*. Grand Rapids: Zondervan, 1976.

Lindsey, Hal, with C. C. Carlson. *The Late Great Planet Earth*. Grand Rapids: Zondervan, 1970.

Miller, J. Keith. *The Taste of New Wine*. Waco, TX: Word, 1965.

Morgan, Marable. *The Total Woman*. Grand Rapids: Fleming Revell, 1973.

Schuller, Robert H. *Move Ahead with Possibility Thinking*. Old Tappan, NJ: Fleming Revell, 1975.

Wallis, Jim. *The Call to Conversion*. San Francisco: Harper & Row, 1981.

ROBERT HUDSON

Of Octavos and Octothorpes: Old Print Tech Casts a New Spell

THE RUMBLINGS BEGAN AROUND 2004. At first they were quiet, almost like distant thunder, but even before I could grasp what was going on, a full-blown tectonic shift had taken place.

Starting in 1986, and for more than thirty years thereafter, I helped organize the editorial internship program for Zondervan. Structuring it much like a college-level course, I taught ten class sessions over as many weeks, focusing on the proofreading and editing of manuscripts, so that students learned, in the words of medieval monk and bibliophile Richard de Bury, how to "smooth the pathway before the reader." The interns also learned about manuscript review, marketing, author relations, and acquisitions, and listened to a brief history of Christian publishing. Aside from offering them manuscripts on which to practice, I included in my classes written homework and assigned readings from a small syllabus of editing- and publishing-related texts.

The class size was ideal: always one or occasionally two college-age students per semester. They hailed from a wide variety of schools. During the school year, they most often came from Calvin College (now Calvin University), though I occasionally worked with students from Grand Valley State University and Cornerstone University. During the summer months, students arrived from farther afield, from colleges like Houghton, Oberlin, Taylor, Michigan State, and others. Before I retired in 2018, this program had become the favorite part of my job, for I discovered within myself a passion for training the next generation of Christian editors.

On the first day of each semester, the incoming intern was asked to make a sort of get-to-know-you presentation. She (and I say *she* because of the more than seventy interns I supervised, all but three were women) was required to report on her five favorite "culture heroes," the writers, artists, musicians, and thinkers who had most shaped her life. Three times out of four these college-age women, nearly all of whom were English majors, would include Jane Austen on their lists. While J. R. R. Tolkien and C. S. Lewis made frequent appearances, with occasional cameos by Shakespeare, Louisa May Alcott, and the Brontës, Austen was a constant, a polestar that seemed to have guided many of these women to literature.

But that began to change in 2004—the year in which the first wave of students who had been read Harry Potter at an impressionable age began to apply for internships. Almost overnight, Jane Austen was eclipsed by J. K. Rowling in the pantheon of the immortals. Over the next fourteen years, Austen's name was mentioned only once more, and even then, she was ranked a slot or two below Rowling.

For the most part, I welcomed the shift. Life is change, and such sudden storms tend to refresh the air. In fact, I'd been an avid Harry Potter fan myself even before he became an international phenomenon. Having read in *Booklist* how popular the books were becoming in the UK, I purchased Scholastic's US edition the week it was released in September of 1998. Rowling's gift of invention was clearly one of the greatest of the last century, second only to Tolkien's; and, as the glossy magazines widely reported, she did indeed encourage a generation of young people—even children—to read. Seven-year-olds were suddenly breezing through books that were as hefty as anything found on the average college 101 syllabus.

The interns' other culture heroes began to fade as well. While Tolkien and Lewis still popped up, classic literary figures grew more sparse. Shakespeare and the Brontës were replaced by a new wave of young adult novelists, contemporary fantasy writers, cartoonists, popular filmmakers, bloggers, and anime artists.

This shift was so thorough that it seemed an aberration when one young woman bucked the trend by declaring Mary Wollstonecraft's *Vindication of the Rights of Woman* as the most influential book in her life. The exception that proved the rule. Otherwise, there was a dearth of writers from what English professors used to call "the canon."

This shift had nothing to do with lack of education. Inspired by Rowling and an array of popular young writers, these interns were intent upon becoming book editors. Books had captured their imagination. By and large, this new crop of students were sharp observers and wry conversationalists; they were keenly intelligent, well-read, and brighter than I'd been at their age. Like English majors everywhere, they were familiar with "the canon," but I was surprised by how little influence it had on their lives.

The explanation, of course, was that these students were not just the first generation to encounter Harry Potter, they were the first generation to grow up on the Internet. The problem was *not* that they didn't know the past; rather, they perceived it differently. They were less reverential toward its towering monuments, and less deferential to its ancient authority. Living as they did in an age in which the entire culture was hyperaware that something new and unprecedented was taking place, these students simply felt that the past had limited relevance to their lives. To them, the language of classic book culture was a second language. Their primary tongue was Internet—and more specifically, social media. My interns tended to see themselves less as part of the grand flow of history, and more as standing at the headwaters of global change.

Life, as I said, is change . . . and this change led me to a marvelous discovery. An unprecedented opportunity lay before me, one that brought about a counterintuitive redirection to the way I trained and mentored the interns. I sensed that these students were beginning to view words—the whole enterprise of language—as something that was ethereal, something that when reduced to pixels and dwelling in the ether of the digital cosmos, seemed to exist apart from the material world. They were slowly losing sight of the vast crowd of people, living and dead, who were involved in the production of every book: not just the writers and editors, but the designers and typographers, binders and printers, artists and craftspeople, sales and marketing teams. Literature is not simply a cerebral activity. Rather, every letter on every page had to have been painstakingly crafted by someone at some time; every page, in fact, had to be manufactured, as did the cloth of the cover, the foil of spine titling, the inks and the glue, the thread and the headbands. Books are the product of a community.

So instead of reckoning with the new, I zealously embraced the old. I gambled that what these students most needed was a thorough immersion in the basics—and by *basics* I mean the nitty-gritty, hands-on, fundamentals of print books—their creation, their traditions and customs, their history, and ultimately their foundational relevance to the digital age.

I began with paper, the physical object itself. In one of the first class sessions of each semester, I had the interns make paper, from paper molds dipped by hand into tubs of pulp-infused water. This gave us the opportunity to discuss the history of paper and how the technology of paper paralleled—even drove—the course of book history. We learned the names of the great papermakers. While paper is now produced on huge machines, our small sheets of handmade paper allowed the students to see how deckled edges were created, how watermarks were made, and how different ingredients in the pulp affected the print quality of the finished page.

We then looked at the basics of signature construction by actually taking sheets of paper, nesting them together, and folding them to the appropriate sizes: one-fold folios (coffee-table size books), two-fold quartos (trade size), and three-fold octavos (mass-market size). I demonstrated the complicated technique for creating signatures that displayed twelve pages to a side of paper (duodecimo), a fold that is commonly used in the production of gift books. With nothing but a bone folder, a pair of scissors, and a single heavy staple, we even made miniature 128-page, postage-stamp-size books out of a single sheet of paper. It can be done. Signature construction allowed the students to become aware of the complex science of page imposition and the importance of recto and verso placements.

This led to a consideration of binding techniques (sewn, perfect bound, case bound, and others), and we examined, in detail, how physical books are made—by reversing the process. Just as science students dissect frogs, we dissected actual books with an X-Acto knife so we could study their binding, their cover and spine materials, and their manufacture and durability.

Using cold metal type, we looked at how books used to be set and printed by hand, and this, in turn, gave the interns the opportunity to delve into the history of letterforms, from the Roman capitals of the Trajan column to the latest digitized fonts, including the one called *Trajan*, which duplicates the ancient Roman letters. We looked at the history of typography and page design, and how font size, leading, margins, word-per-line counts, and word and letter spacing affect readability. Each student was required to study in depth one typeface and type designer. Then we examined readability formulas like the one developed by Flesch.

In addition to teaching about the material dimensions of publishing, I stressed the importance of knowing the technical language of not just editing and proofreading—which was mandatory to start with—but of production, printing, design, and typography. Did they know, for instance, how computer points and picas relate to old-style points and picas? Did they know the origins of such common terms as *lowercase, leading, italic, galley,* and so many more? Did they know the difference between a *page number* and a *folio*? Did they know that the beloved hashtag symbol used on Twitter actually has a name other than *the number sign* or *the pound sign*? Some typographers of the previous century referred to it as *the octothorpe.*

My new approach engaged the interns in a satisfyingly profound way. These students, whose lives had been shaped by fantasy literature, suddenly found that the millennia-old lore of bookmaking became a fantasy world in itself, filled with vibrant, almost wizard-like characters, from Aldus Manutius (who virtually created the Renaissance with such innovative editions as his *Metamorphoses* of Ovid in 1502) to William Morris (who produced one of the most magisterial books in history, his *Works of Geoffrey Chaucer* in 1896). Morris, by the way, was himself a major writer of fantasy novels— and Manutius published his share of dream-vision stories as well. What amazed them was that these fantastic characters actually lived. The world of bookmaking was a world of alchemical formulas (like the chart of signature breaks or the Flesch Readability Quotient) and arcane knowledge (the imposition of a sixteen-page signature and the secret name for the hashtag). They began to understand that bookmaking is a form of divination, of magic.

These sessions offered the interns a powerful vision of their own place in the grand sweep of book history. In becoming editors and proofreaders, they were becoming part of a traditional craft that reached back thousands of years, a tradition that was always reinventing itself. They saw, perhaps for the first time, that even J. K. Rowling was part of a great and age-old tradition, that she could not have written the Harry Potter books at all if she had not herself been Hermione Granger at heart, someone who revered and loved old books and the people who made them and knew that all the wisdom in the world was contained in them. And Hermione knew a thing or two about magic.

If the course connected interns with the past, I think, on a more practical note, it also shed light on how traditional book culture is the foundation upon which digital text content is built. Indeed, in the early days of the Internet, pages were dreary and unpleasant affairs, difficult to look at, made up of letters with coarse pixelations. Only as web pages began to incorporate more readable, traditional fonts and pleasing designs did they become accessible to the average person. Readability is still readability, whatever the format.

My new approach was, in part, an effort to resist the increasing mechanization of the publishing process, the tendency to view bookmaking as an assembly line rather than a craft. The editor, instead of overseeing the aesthetic integrity of the entire process, was becoming a cog in the larger machine. As master editor Judith Markham once wrote, an editor should be like the conductor of an orchestra. The conductor doesn't necessarily need to know how to play every instrument, but the conductor needs to know enough about each instrument to be able to create a coherent harmony. Likewise, an editor needs to know enough about every stage of the process to give artistic cohesiveness to the production of each book.

All of this training gave the interns a new confidence as they began their careers in publishing. It seemed they had crossed a threshold into a new maturity, into a perspective on books beyond fantasy novels and social media. Ultimately, the key was learning the language of publishing as well as its history so they could speak it as a native. This language would prove invaluable as they began their interviews with prospective employers. Knowing it meant that they could ask a publisher intelligent questions not just about their editorial house style and proofreading standards, but also about their typographic, design, binding, paper, and readability standards.

More than a dozen former interns now work for publishing houses, and several others are highly respected editorial freelancers. The woman who listed Mary Wollstonecraft as her favorite author is now on the editorial staff of a major publishing house. Of course, the students of this Harry Potter generation would have achieved great things even without their internship experience, because each brought an eagerness and a vast capacity to learn that would have helped them excel no matter what they did or where they went.

Perhaps most gratifying of all was that their immersion in the traditional craft of books sometimes made a profound difference in small and unexpected ways. For instance, one of the interns, who went on to become an assistant children's book editor at a major New York publisher, wrote a poem as a way of saying farewell to me and the internship. Never had an intern written a poem for me before. I was overwhelmed.

Her poem was titled "Octothorpe."

JON STOCK

On the Early Days of Wipf and Stock

JOHN WIPF AND I are merely a couple of used book dealers. In the fall of 1995 I approached John, suggesting that we might be able to use emerging digital technology to reprint classic books in biblical studies and theology. My vision, originally, was to simply reprint rare books within the public domain. Our first two publications were John Henry Newman's *Arians in the Fourth Century* and a collection of essays by P. T. Forsyth, drawn from various sources, headlined by "Divine Self-Emptying."

Jim Tedrick was the first employee we hired. He started out using Optical Character Recognition software on the books at a tiny desk in the back of our bookshop, running a copier in the basement of the house we shared, and binding and cutting books in Jim's bedroom. In all, Wipf and Stock Publishers started from very humble origins.

The genesis of reprinting books still under copyright protection began with cold calling T. F. Torrance on his fiftieth wedding anniversary. I was hoping to reprint Torrance's *Doctrine of Grace in the Apostolic Fathers*, as it was a slender book that commanded a $45 price in the used market. We figured that, if we could reprint it for $15, we could sell one hundred copies—a pretty modest agenda back in the nineties. The Torrance connection proved essential to us. At our very first American Academy of Religion and Society of Biblical Literature (AAR/SBL) conference in San Francisco, 1997, we had one booth back in the corner. All of our covers were a powder blue card stock, since that was the only style that could hold toner, so the booth contained little to catch the eye. Yet, Alan Sell and Don McKim happened by. Both were prolific authors with a number of out-of-print books. Seeing that we were publishing Torrance piqued their interest and we began a publishing relationship with them as well, which led to further networks and on and on . . . our reprint business boomed.

It was not until a couple of Fuller Seminary professors, Dean Gilliland and Colin Brown, approached John Wipf about reprinting a couple of their own books that we realized there was a need in the mid-nineties for on-demand academic reprinting. We found no shortage of professors who did not want to change their syllabi merely because their book had gone out of print. So we hired a series of part-time employees who spent their days calling all the college bookstores for schools listed in the Association of Theological Schools guide. We would call each bookstore manager and suggest to them that, if a professor requested a textbook that was out of print, they could contact us and we would negotiate reprint rights and fulfill the order. This was a boon to us and probably saved our business in the late nineties.

Early on, we were approached for special new book projects by various authors who were having a hard time finding a publisher, but as we rolled into the new millennium, it became apparent that if we were to continue to survive, and maybe even grow, we would need to invest in moving beyond reprints to developing our own new publications. Lighting Source was approaching every publisher in the country trying to get them to sign on to their digital printing program. As a division of Ingram, the largest book distributor in the country, they had a substantial advantage over Wipf and Stock in enticing publishers to find a digital future for their backlist or previously out-of-print works. The writing was on the wall: we needed to develop our own fresh intellectual property or accept that we would hit a growth ceiling. Like several before us (Kregel, Baker), we moved from being a reprint house to establishing our own new publication divisions.

As we expanded into new publications in the early 2000s, we knew we were going to have a challenge finding an editor to lead us. I had no idea what budget we could afford, so I emailed several senior editors I knew from other publishing houses, asking if they could recommend a junior editor who might be a good fit for what we wanted to do. One of those editors was K. C. Hanson of Fortress Press. K. C. and I had a history; we had worked together in a sawmill in the late 1970s (go figure!). We were more than shocked when K. C. indicated that he himself might be interested in taking the position. K. C. and his wife, Alice, flew out to interview. We agreed to pay him more than we could afford, and the rest is history. K. C. had a PhD from Claremont, an extensive teaching history, and a career at one of the most important biblical/theological publishing houses. He gave us immediate legitimacy in a number of circles, brought new book publishing experience (of which we had little), and he created our house style.

K. C.'s specialty was biblical studies, especially Ancient Near East and social scientific approaches to Scripture. We knew that we were going to need to find other specialists and reached out to friends in the academic community who might connect us with young PhDs in search of work. Stanley Hauerwas was quick to recommend Charlie Collier, who had done his dissertation under him. Charlie brought an inquisitive mind, a dogged attitude, and has filled out our theology and ethics program since he came aboard in July of 2006.

Our next hire came about as the result of a small AAR/SBL wine party that we used to co-host with Loyola New Testament scholar Steve Fowl. In 1993, at the Washington, DC AAR/SBL, James Stock and I retreated from the main party to watch some football. We were joined by the most amiable Texan you'll ever meet. Chris Spinks had done his dissertation at Fuller Seminary on the debates over the theological interpretation of scripture (including extended reference to the aforementioned Fowl). It took James and I about thirty minutes to conclude that Chris would be a perfect fit for our team. He has been the picture of consistency for us since 1994.

Those three gentlemen were our core team, building Cascade and Pickwick for a number of years. And then we began to bring in our friends.

We first met Robin Parry at AAR/SBL in Atlanta in 1986, and we offered him a job in 1987. But Robin already had a job as the director of Paternoster Press. We remained great friends over the years, and when Paternoster was sold we convinced him to come on board with us. Robin just might be the nicest hardworking editor on the planet. Even those who disagree with his universalism find him undeniably charming.

Rodney Clapp and I were introduced by Greg Jones (formerly dean at Duke Divinity School), way back at that first AAR/SBL in 1997 when Rodney was still working for InterVarsity Press and had yet to co-found Brazos Press. Our friendship was cemented by a road trip through the Delta Blues country, from New Orleans to Chicago. Said friendship has only grown over the years, and it is a joy to work with him. Rodney reads across the disciplines with an astute eye and fills a gap that long needed filling.

Both Robin and Rodney have extensive lists of their own publications, each with great diversity.

Michael Thompson is our final (or most recent) piece of the puzzle. We first offered Michael a job in 1996, and, while interested, he turned us down. He was, after all, moving up at Eerdmans Publishing, one of the most respected names in our business. Nevertheless, we maintained our friendship over the years. He would join us occasionally to shoot pool, sit around the table at the bar, go out to dinner—all the while consuming his ever-present Diet Coke. While Michael has been with us for less than a year, his work ethic is astounding (I get 3 AM emails from him) and many an author can testify that Michael is relentless when pursuing a book. We are lucky to have him. We are lucky to have our entire editorial staff.

I hope you can see the ethos here, one word: friendship. Our editors do not compete, they do not wrangle. They are friends and partners—this is an essential element of the new publishing culture.

One other word I may include here is *freedom*. Our entire publishing program for Cascade and Pickwick Publications is built around our editors. They and they alone determine what gets published in these imprints. Unlike at many publishing companies, they do not have finance or marketing looking over their shoulder. Our editors are not forced to speculate what unit sales may be. We want them to have the freedom to publish based on their own assessment of a project's merit.

From the beginning our approach to publishing, whether it be a reprint or a new publication, is that "it is all about relationships; the author is our customer." Granted, as we've grown, we probably don't do as well as we used to. It was much easier to keep our ideal when we had one hundred authors; we now have approximately 9,000 authors, editors, and contributors across all of our imprints. Regardless, co-owners James Stock, director of marketing, and Jim Tedrick, director of publications, are ultimately accessible to one and all. When you call us, you will not be met by a recorded system (well, unless all the lines are busy!) . . . you will always be met by a human voice. We insist on the personal, especially for our authors (but also for those book buyers who call in), even if it means less profit.

Hospitality is an essential ethos for us. In our building, we rent space to a pizza company and a coffeehouse. Those of us who work at Wipf and Stock gather weekly for food and beverage. The coffeehouse is a central spot for meetings and entertaining guests. When we travel to various conferences around the country (we generally exhibit at around thirty per year), we want to pick up the bar tab. Our business was built first and foremost on entertaining friends and making new friends. We've had a hard-and-fast rule when we settle in at a lounge. All are welcome, and we don't talk business. Occasionally the latter rule gets broken, but, generally, if you (or one of our editors) want to talk business—then an appointment gets set. But, after the conference workday is done, we want to invite each other and all who will join into a world of friendship, camaraderie, and interesting conversation. We've made many friends over the years, some of whom will never publish with us. That may sound odd, but I believe that if a company can stay true to an ethos beyond the bottom line, beyond acquiring the next big project, then it can keep its head held high, even if the ship is going down. As people of faith, we are called to value the personal and the relational above the commercial. By God, I pray that we can maintain this standard.

I should add, and I suspect I might be being too braggadocios when I say it, that our Monday night parties at AAR/SBL have become legendary. Many of our friends stay the extra night into Tuesday, just so they can attend the party. For years, we were unable to afford the standard publisher reception; in fact we usually spent Saturday and Sunday nights crashing the parties of other friends in the industry. We would usually host a Monday night dinner with fifteen to twenty friends and authors, which were wonderful evenings filled with great food, drink, and laughter. When we were finally able to pull off a full reception, we wanted 200 of our good friends and authors to be able to make a night of it with all the food and beverage they desired . . . we wanted them to enjoy a full meal like we had shared with the smaller group in years past. So, we made the leap—and we've had some great times: Buddy Guy's in Chicago, House of Blues in San Diego, Camden Yards in Baltimore (a personal favorite of this baseball fan). These nights are so rewarding. I love standing at the entry point and greeting all of our guests as they come in; authors, old friends, new friends—it is normally a loud, crowded, busy night, and we wouldn't have it any other way.

Our greatest strength is also our greatest weakness. None of us who started and ran the publishing company had ever worked in publishing. Hence, we had no model. We had no guidance for "how things got done." We really did make it up as we went along—K. C. Hanson, when he showed up eleven years into this game, was our first employee with any experience in traditional publishing. By then, we were already set in our ways, often repeating the mantra "just because everyone else does it this way does not mean that we should." We've thrived on being contrarian and trying to approach dilemmas with imagination, resisting the status quo of traditional publishing models (which we still don't know a whole lot about).

Unfortunately, this has limited us in some ways. We've never attended the Frankfurt Book Fair, we've never received grants for funding translations, we don't have any connections at Lilly or any other trust that might fund larger series or publishing projects. We are outsiders who remain ignorant of some very important elements of the publishing industry.

Our somewhat eccentric model is not so appealing to certain established authors or academics with a vision for a particular career track . . . we'll never be Cambridge UP or Brill. What has allowed for our remarkable growth (seemingly out of nowhere for some) also prevents us from being an attractive publishing option for some.

On the other hand, as traditional publishing has retracted, we've been able to provide a home for many who have been squeezed out of their previous publishing homes. Our model has allowed numerous focus groups, authors, and particularistic biblical and theological genres to maintain their work in publishing. Our model allows us to welcome them without worrying over whether a particular academic series or author is able to hit a certain sales benchmark. This has been one of the more rewarding elements of our publishing over the last years, allowing voices of merit to remain in the larger biblical-theological conversation.

I don't think many would dispute that, for many, the old model is suffering in academic religious publishing. It certainly still works for those companies with excellent branding and creative leadership. But it is no secret that the publishing world has changed substantially over the last twenty years, and I firmly believe that the next twenty years will bring even larger changes.

Finally, I must say that what success we've had and will continue to have will have to be credited to Jim Tedrick and James Stock, the two best hires I've ever made. They run Wipf and Stock; it is a joy to solve problems with them. We don't really know the future of religious publishing. We just know that we have to stay nimble, we must think outside the box, and we must maintain the courage to take risks and the humility to hear criticism. But in the end, it is all about relationships.

GREG THORNTON

Publishing God's Glorious Deeds

AN OFFICE MOVE HAS me once again purging files and books, preparing for a new space. I've been spoiled with the number of bookcases and files and drawers in the office I've occupied for the last seven years. Among other things, the move is forcing me to change habits, and to become more "digital," storing information on my laptop or on the organization's cloud network, instead of in a file cabinet or a credenza drawer. It's staggering the volume of paper I've accumulated!

This movement from paper to digital is representative of some of the dramatic changes in publishing in the last forty years. Connecting with others has advanced from hand-typed memos on an electric typewriter, to dictating letters on recorders with mini cassette tapes, to desktop computers connected to printers with faxing capability, to computers with Internet bringing email to life, to texting, to Twitter. Still there's always been the phone.

Even as these advancements have brought changes in personal forms of communication, they've also influenced the dynamics in publishing. *Disruption* is a term often used to describe these sometimes abrupt and significant changes. For publishers, the editorial and production processes have evolved, making publishers much more efficient and productive. In addition, the channels available to get edited books from publishers to readers continues to develop at ever-increasing speed.

All of this means ideas are moving more rapidly from the mind of the author to the eye and ear of the reader. Wise publishers are continually adjusting internal processes in order to capture the advantages offered by these technological advancements. One of the latest advances is audiobooks. A new generation is rising up and "reading" books by listening. Audiobooks allow books to be consumed on the go, whether in the car, biking, or while walking or jogging.

Yet what hasn't changed is the overall mission of Christian publishing. The psalmist writes, "Sing to the LORD; praise his name. Each day proclaim the good news that he saves. Publish his glorious deeds among the nations. Tell everyone about the amazing things he does" (Psalm 96:2, 3 NLT). Christian publishers proclaim the good news that Jesus saves.

This was the reason the evangelist D. L. Moody started the Bible Institute Colportage Association (BICA) in 1894. He launched a publishing company, which continues to this day as Moody Publishers, with four original goals: "First, to help stem the awful tide of impure reading matter that is annually being scattered broadcast, which is poisoning the minds and undermining the characters of all who read it; second, to reach the non-churchgoer; third, to get the printed page into the hands of every criminal behind the prison bars in the United States; fourth, to give an opportunity to godly men or women to do more effective service for the Master, in dealing with individuals in their homes about their soul's salvation."[1]

By God's grace, the publishing program associated with the Moody Bible Institute is in its' 125th year of operation. Though the goals have adjusted a bit, the publishing program is still committed to richly equipping people in the Word of God and supporting the church's work of discipling all people.

For those of us in this noble profession, we have found that Christian publishing easily becomes part of your identity, even though it doesn't usually get the interest of family and friends at parties! Moody Publishers has a rich history of men and women devoting decades to this work. D. L. Moody hired William Norton to direct the operations of the BICA in 1897; Norton served in that role until his death fifty-one years later. MBI Board Chairman at that time, Henry Parsons Crowell (founder of Quaker Oats), called his friend William Norton a quiet, self-effacing man. Norton hired

---

1. During the Civil War, the young D. L. Moody ministered to the Confederate prisoners held at Camp Douglas on Chicago's South Side. Called a true friend of prisoners, Mr. Moody frequently visited jails even after the Civil War. He had a heart to reach those imprisoned with Bibles, books, and tracts, seeking to win these prisoners to Christ. Years later, with the forming of the BICA, he started a book fund, personally raising most of the money, to send free-of-charge books, Scripture portions, and gospel tracts to chaplains and religious workers for distribution in penitentiaries, prisons, jails, and reform schools. Getz, *MBI*, 136–37.

a young Roy Granzow, who served for more than fifty years. Roy kept all of the business records for Moody Press when I started in 1981, about the time this information was being moved from paper files and index cards onto the MBI mainframe. Like William Norton, Roy Granzow was another quiet, loyal, and committed worker. Roy Granzow overlapped with revered directors of the publishing operation; individuals like Ken Taylor, Harold Shaw, Pete Gunther, and Jerry Jenkins. Moreover, this past year we recognized the retirement of another colleague with more than fifty years of faithful service.

These wise and gifted individuals not only devoted themselves to the publishing work at Moody, they also supported the wider cause of global Christian publishing. In 1950, then director of Moody Press and later founder of Tyndale House Publishers, Dr. Ken Taylor, and another Moody Press employee, William Moore, were involved in the start of the Christian Booksellers Association. Ken Taylor and Pete Gunther were also involved in 1953 in establishing Evangelical Literature Overseas, a service agency to evangelical groups to foster inter-mission cooperation. That work was eventually taken up by Media Associates International when this new organization launched in 1985. MAI is flourishing today under the fine leadership of John Maust.

As the publishing arm of The Moody Bible Institute, Moody Publishers has as its' mission to provide high-quality, thought-provoking books and products that connect truth to real needs and challenges, and to help fund the training of Moody Bible Institute students, who carry the gospel to every corner of the world. Ken Taylor was interviewed for the one-hundredth anniversary celebration of the publishing house in 1994. Dr. Taylor said that among his accomplishments, he was grateful that Moody Press was profitable. At the same time, Moody Press was performing a wonderful service to the Christian public. It grew and formed a solid base for its later rapid extension in the 1960s and seventies. Many authors were, and still are, attracted to this twofold mission, and choose to publish with Moody. Today more than 1,500 full-time undergrad students are enrolled at the Moody Bible Institute in Chicago, with their tuition sponsored by generous donors, along with proceeds generated from Moody Publishers.

Moody Publishers is known as a backlist-driven house, meaning a larger percentage of the annual sales are from titles more than one year old. Publishing involves risk, as there's no guarantee that new titles will sell to projections. Yet sales of backlist titles are more predictable, as they found an identifiable and reachable readership.

One of the more significant backlist categories at Moody are reference works, like the *Unger's Bible Dictionary* and *Unger's Bible Handbook*. Both titles, written by Dallas Seminary professor Merrill Unger, were published originally in the 1960s. New four-color editions were produced of both books in the eighties with help from Angus Hudson, a UK-based publisher that specialized in co-editions, making it possible for the simultaneous release of economical editions of the same book in multiple languages, by different publishers. More than fifty years later, these two reference books by Dr. Unger, with combined sales of more than 1.7 million, continue to help readers in their study of the Bible. Moody Publishers was proud to launch a new reference work in 2014, *The Moody Bible Commentary*. Almost seven years in the making, this one-volume Bible commentary has more than 1.5 million words (most popular-level books have less than 60,000 words) and almost 2,200 pages. Thirty Moody Bible Institute professors contributed to it. It's also been a huge privilege to partner with Dr. John MacArthur over a thirty-year period to publish the thirty-four volume *MacArthur New Testament Commentary*. This life work of John MacArthur has been a trusted resource for students of the Bible, and has been translated into multiple languages.

Publishing, even with advances in production and print technology, still has relatively long lead times. Our friends at Moody Radio talk about radio being like a racehorse, publishing like a turtle when comparing the speed to market with messages! The publishing normal is to sign new projects based upon a written proposal, with a manuscript delivered in six to twenty-four months, as most Christian authors have other full-time jobs and only write evenings and weekends. Then another six months are needed for editing, typesetting, proofreading, and printing.

Yet there are times when more expediency is needed. For example, it was invigorating for the Moody Publishers team to address concerns Christians had around two controversial films, *The Last Temptation of Christ* in 1988, and *The DaVinci Code* in 2006. Dr. Erwin Lutzer quickly researched and wrote *The Last Temptation of Christ: Its Deception and What You Should Do About It*, and the booklet was published in 1988 as the film was released. Dr. Lutzer was a frequent guest on radio shows covering the controversy. Years later in 2006, Moody Bible Institute president Michael Easley worked with John Ankerberg and Dillon Burroughs to write the book, *The Da Vinci Code Controversy: 10 Facts You Should Know*. Though these fast-track projects required heroic efforts on the part of the authors and the publishing staff, all believed that the gain was worth the pain when we saw the feedback from readers.

Christian publishing is populated with generous leaders who graciously and willingly give of their time to mentor others. I have been the beneficiary of wise and talented individuals who kindly shared their expertise in formal and informal ways. At various stages of my career, counsel from Jerry Jenkins, Pete Gunther, Angus Hudson, Kent Puckett, Joe Ragont, John Bass, Bob Reekie, Bill Anderson, Dennis Shere, Larry Mercer, Ed Cannon, Tony Evans, Robert Wolgemuth, and Nancy DeMoss Wolgemuth provided much needed knowledge, inspiration, and hope. I am deeply appreciative for these who shared of themselves so freely. Now I seek to do the same.

I'm also grateful to have had the opportunity to work with some of God's choicest servants. Christian publishing connects publishers with men and women uniquely gifted by God, who possess expertise and unique communication skills. Some of my most memorable moments in publishing are of conversations with these men and women, usually around a conference or restaurant table, discussing not only a new book project, yet more, what God is teaching them in their walk with him. Many of these authors have become dear friends and co-laborers, as we have bonded through our love for Jesus Christ, and the desire to see his kingdom come on earth as it is in heaven. And with a few, these conversations have carried over into their homes, and relationships established with whole families. I've even been privileged to walk with some to the end of their days, and carry treasured memories of our friendship. J. Oswald Sanders, Larry Burkett, and Charles Ryrie come to mind. All three are now with the Lord, even as their writings continue to equip and inspire new generations of readers.

An honest essay on Christian publishing wouldn't be complete without mention of the sting of poor publishing decisions. Many titles don't perform to expectations, for a variety of reasons. Usually it's more than simply ineffective packaging or marketing, both of which are extremely important. Well-written, relevant content, packaged and priced well, will find a reading audience, regardless of the size of the marketing budget. We've learned the hard way to have a "setting-the-expectations" conversation with authors, especially first-time authors. Publishers continually balance optimism with realism.

Yet some of the most valuable lessons I've had in publishing have come from times when titles I didn't accept for publication went on to become helpful, widely sold books through another publisher. I remember one proposal was on a timely topic, written from a biblically based approach by an expert in the field. The proposal itself was poorly written. But rather than seeing beyond the proposal to what could be, I rejected the book. Another publisher, with vision to see what could be, matched the expert author with a talented writer, and effectively packaged and sold hundreds of thousands of copies. This was an important point to remember: publishers must sometimes look beyond the proposal as submitted to what could be. Interestingly, this author later became a colleague at Moody, and we were able to laugh about my poor decision.

I learned as well from rejecting a project from one of our best-selling authors. This title was intended for an audience Moody wasn't sure would respond to a book, even if written by this well-known author. Again another publisher (interestingly, the same one that picked up the other rejected project I mentioned above), worked in harmony with this author to create a masterfully packaged and written title that became this author's all-time leading bestseller. This author, who happens to be a good friend, now "kindly" likes to remind me of Moody's missed opportunity!

Almost all of the titles published by Moody these 125 years have carried the Moody name on the spine. Yet in 1992, the Northfield imprint was launched. At that time, buyers at a number of the leading chain bookstores had a bias against "religious" books, and limited the number of nonfiction titles from religious publishers like Moody. It was perceived there wasn't an audience for these overtly religious books filled with Bible quotes. With the help of a handful of willing and capable authors, the Northfield imprint was launched (Northfield, Massachusetts is the birthplace of D. L. Moody). Titles in this imprint were designed to reach non-Christians with relevant books on contemporary issues. The principles presented were all biblical, yet presented without references to the Bible chapter and verse. The books were intended to prepare readers for the truth of the gospel and salvation in Jesus Christ. The first titles in the imprint included the *Family Budget Workbook* by Christian financial expert Larry Burkett, and *The Stress Factor* by counselors Paul Minirth and Frank Meier. A few months later *The Five Love Languages* by Dr. Gary Chapman was published. Since its release in 1992, this incredibly helpful book has reached more than twelve million English-speaking readers, and has been translated into more than fifty languages. In the book, Gary briefly tells the story of how he rediscovered his need for God, and how by examining the historical accounts of Christ's birth, life, death, and resurrection, he came to view Christ's death as an expression of God's love. He encourages readers to make their own investigation of these truths.

Then in 1999, the Lift Every Voice Books imprint was launched as a partnership with Dr. Matthew Parker and the Institute for Black Family Development. Books in this imprint explore issues facing the African American community through nonfiction and fiction titles written by and for African Americans. Since 1990, Moody Publishers (and Lift Every Voice Books) has published eighty titles by twenty-seven African American authors.

Mergers and acquisitions are quite common in Christian publishing. Though Moody has not been an active participant in this arena, we were pleased in 2013 to acquire Wingspread Publishers, which included titles by A. W. Tozer (Tozer accounted for fifty-seven of the 138 titles acquired). Readers have responded well to this acquisition, especially church and ministry leaders. Moody has been able to carry on and even expand the readership of this legacy author. We've added a number of new compilations of Tozer's writings and are seeing an increasing number of readers benefit from Tozer's work.

God has used the written word to inspire and instruct his church for thousands of years. Even with the great changes and disruptions the last forty years, the future is very bright for readers and publishers in the future. A friend said to me when I first started in Christian publishing that the best Christian books have yet to be written. I believe he was, and still is, right. The church needs more books that inform, educate, and inspire and that help all of us serve Christ more effectively. Until Christ returns, there will be an ever-increasing number in his global church eager to read and learn more about our great God.

The verse inscribed on the arch leading from LaSalle Boulevard onto the campus at the Moody Bible Institute is 2 Timothy 2:15: "Study to shew thyself approved unto God, a workman that needeth not to be ashamed, rightly dividing the word of truth" (King James Version). Publishing does just that: providing resources that strengthen and encourage the global body of believers. It's been a high honor to serve God as a Christian publisher. One of my favorite prayers for Moody Publishers is Psalm 90:17: "Let the favor of the LORD our God be upon us; and confirm the work of our hands; yes, confirm the work of our hands." As those associated with this historic publishing ministry continue to seek to honor Christ in all, I believe God will hear and answer this prayer.

BIBLIOGRAPHY

Getz, Gene A. *MBI: The Story of The Moody Bible Institute.* Chicago: Moody, 1969.